AF528799

SOFTWARE TESTING

THE AUTHORS

Mrs. P. Vanitha has received M.E. degree in Computer Science and Engineering from Anna University, Chennai. Currently she is working as an Assistant Professor in Department of Information Technology, Kongu Engineering College, Erode, and Tamilnadu, India. She is having 14 years of experience in Teaching. She always engaged to fill the gap between the students and industry with latest technologies. She is the lifetime member in International Association of Engineers. So far she has published 21 research papers in various National, International Conferences and Journals. Her area of interest is Data Mining, Networking and Software Engineering.

Mrs. R. Aarthi has received Bachelor's degree in Information Technology and Masters degree in Computer Science and Engineering from Anna University, Chennai. Pursuing her Ph.D in Medical Datamining under Anna University, Chennai. She is having 13 years of teaching experience. Currently she is working as Assistant professor in the department of Information Technology at Kongu Engineering College, Perundurai. She is the lifetime member in Computer society of India. She is basically an Academician, Author and a Researcher. Her current research interests include Data Mining, Machine Learning, Deep Learning, Big data. She is the author/co-author of various Scopus indexed journals and conferences.

Mrs. D. Mohanapriya has received M.E. degree in Computer Science and Engineering from Anna University, Chennai. Currently she is working as an Assistant Professor in Department of Computer Science and Engineering, Nandha College of Technology, Erode, Tamilnadu, India. She is having 14 years of experience in Teaching. She is the lifetime member in Computer Society of India. So far she has published research papers in various National, International Conferences and Journals. Her area of interest is Networking,Deep Learning and Machine learning.

SOFTWARE TESTING

Mrs. P. Vanitha
B.E., M.E., Assistant Professor,
Department of Information Technology,
Kongu Engineering College, Perundurai.

Mrs. R. Aarthi
B.Tech., M.E., Assistant Professor,
Department of Information Technology,
Kongu Engineering College, Perundurai.

Mrs. D. Mohanapriya
B.E., M.E., Assistant Professor,
Department of Computer Science and Engineering,
Nandha College of Technology, Erode.

2026

Daya Publishing House®
A Division of
Astral International Pvt. Ltd.
New Delhi – 110 002

© 2026 AUTHORS

ISBN: 978-93-5919-217-8

Publisher's Note:

Every possible effort has been made to ensure that the information contained in this book is accurate at the time of going to press, and the publisher and author cannot accept responsibility for any errors or omissions, however caused. No responsibility for loss or damage occasioned to any person acting, or refraining from action, as a result of the material in this publication can be accepted by the editor, the publisher or the author. The Publisher is not associated with any product or vendor mentioned in the book. The contents of this work are intended to further general scientific research, understanding and discussion only. Readers should consult with a specialist where appropriate.

Every effort has been made to trace the owners of copyright material used in this book, if any. The author and the publisher will be grateful for any omission brought to their notice for acknowledgement in the future editions of the book.

All Rights reserved under International Copyright Conventions. No part of this publication may be reproduced, stored in a retrieval system, or transmitted in any form or by any means, electronic, mechanical, photocopying, recording or otherwise without the prior written consent of the publisher and the copyright owner.

Published by : **Daya Publishing House®**
A Division of
Astral International Pvt. Ltd.
– ISO 9001:2015 Certified Company –
4736/23, Ansari Road, Darya Ganj
New Delhi-110 002
Ph. 011-43549197, 8130496929
E-mail: info@astralint.com
Website: www.astralint.com

Printed at : **Replika Press Pvt. Ltd.**

PREFACE

Software testing is a critical aspect of software development that ensures the quality and reliability of applications. It encompasses various testing approaches, including manual and automated testing, to identify defects and validate functionality against requirements. Essential features of the testing process include systematic planning, execution, and reporting, which are guided by fundamental principles such as early detection of defects and continuous improvement. A well-defined testing process not only enhances product quality but also minimizes costs associated with post-release defects, emphasizing the importance of effective test methodologies and a skilled testing team. In addition to understanding the testing process, software testers must be aware of the challenges they face, including rapid technological changes and the need for effective collaboration within cross-functional teams. The cost of testing can vary significantly based on project scope and complexity; thus, organizations must strategically allocate resources to achieve optimal outcomes. Test methodologies play a vital role in categorizing defects and ensuring comprehensive coverage during testing phases. Furthermore, testers should possess a diverse skill set that includes analytical thinking, attention to detail, and familiarity with various testing tools to effectively identify issues and communicate findings.

Creating a supportive software testing environment is crucial for fostering team competency and enhancing user satisfaction. This involves establishing clear guidelines for the testing process and providing adequate resources to support testing activities. The seven-step software testing process serves as a framework for organizing testing efforts, from planning through execution to result analysis. By building an effective testing environment that promotes collaboration and continuous learning, organizations can improve their overall software quality while equipping testers with the necessary skills to adapt to evolving industry demands.

To solidify their understanding, students are tasked with a case study involving the creation of a test suite using Selenium IDE that contains at least four test cases. They will conduct tests on two specified websites and write a program to log in to a particular web page. This hands-on experience is designed to enhance their practical skills in using Selenium for automated testing and to familiarize them with real-world applications of software testing tools. By integrating theoretical knowledge with practical application, students will be better equipped to navigate the complexities of software testing in various environments.

Mrs. P. Vanitha

Mrs. R. Aarthi

Mrs. D. Mohanapriya

CONTENTS

UNIT 1

BASICS OF SOFTWARE TESTING

1.1 Introduction

Discover the essence of software testing—a crucial discipline ensuring the reliability and excellence of every software product. This book unveils the principles, techniques, and strategies essential for crafting robust, bug-free applications. Dive into the world of testing methodologies, from unit tests to acceptance criteria, and learn how each step contributes to delivering flawless software.

1.2.Definition

Software testing is a critical process in the software development lifecycle that involves evaluating and verifying that a software application or system meets specified requirements and functions correctly. This systematic process aims to ensure the quality and reliability of the software by identifying defects, bugs, or any deviations from the expected behavior.

- **Identify Defects:** One of the main goals of software testing is to detect and document defects or bugs in the software. Early identification of these issues helps in addressing them before the software is released, reducing the risk of failure in real-world usage.
- **Ensure Quality:** Quality assurance is a fundamental aspect of software testing. It involves assessing various attributes of the software, such as functionality, performance, security, and usability. High-quality software meets or exceeds user expectations and industry standards, leading to greater user satisfaction and fewer post-release issues.
- **Verify Performance:** Software testing also involves verifying that the software performs as expected under different conditions. This includes testing for performance under normal and peak loads, ensuring that the software can handle real-world usage scenarios effectively.

- **Validation and Verification:** Testing verifies that the software does what it is supposed to do (validation) and does it correctly according to the specified requirements (verification). This dual focus ensures that the software is both functional and aligned with user needs and specifications.
- **Risk Management:** By identifying potential issues early, software testing helps in mitigating risks associated with software failures. This proactive approach reduces the likelihood of costly post-release fixes and enhances the overall stability and reliability of the software.

1.3.Testing Approaches

Software testing encompasses various approaches, each designed to address different aspects of the software development lifecycle. These approaches ensure comprehensive coverage and help in identifying issues at different stages of development. The primary testing approaches include:

1. **Manual Testing:** Manual testing involves human testers executing test cases without the aid of automation tools. Testers follow predefined steps to check whether the software behaves as expected. This approach is particularly useful for:

- **Exploratory Testing:** Testers explore the software without predefined test cases to discover defects.
- **Usability Testing:** Evaluating the user interface and overall user experience.
- **Ad-hoc Testing:** Informal testing without a structured plan, relying on the tester's understanding and experience.

2. **Automated Testing:** Automated testing uses specialized tools to execute pre-scripted tests on the software. This approach is ideal for repetitive, time-consuming tasks and ensures consistent and accurate test execution. Key benefits include:

- **Regression Testing:** Ensuring that new code changes do not adversely affect existing functionalities.
- **Performance Testing:** Assessing software performance under various conditions using tools to simulate load.
- **Functional Testing:** Verifying that specific functions of the software work as intended.

3. **Black Box Testing:** In black box testing, testers evaluate the software without knowledge of its internal code structure. They focus on input and output, ensuring the software behaves correctly from the user's perspective. Common techniques include:

- **Equivalence Partitioning:** Dividing input data into equivalent partitions to reduce the number of test cases.

- **Boundary Value Analysis:** Testing at the boundaries between partitions to identify edge cases.
- **Decision Table Testing:** Using decision tables to represent combinations of inputs and their corresponding outputs.

4. **White Box Testing:** White box testing, also known as clear box testing, involves testing the internal structures and workings of the software. Testers have access to the source code and use this knowledge to design test cases. Techniques include:

- **Statement Coverage:** Ensuring that each line of code is executed at least once.
- **Branch Coverage:** Testing each possible branch in the control flow.
- **Path Coverage:** Ensuring all possible paths through the code are tested.

5. **Grey Box Testing:** Grey box testing combines elements of both black box and white box testing. Testers have partial knowledge of the internal structures but focus primarily on the software's behavior. This approach helps identify issues that are not apparent through black box testing alone.

6. **Static Testing:** Static testing involves reviewing the software's code, documentation, and design without executing the code. This approach aims to identify defects early in the development process. Techniques include:

- **Code Reviews:** Peer reviews of the source code to identify errors and improvements.
- **Static Analysis:** Using automated tools to analyze code for potential issues.

7. **Dynamic Testing:** Dynamic testing involves executing the software and observing its behavior. This approach is used to validate the software's functionality, performance, and usability. It includes:

- **Functional Testing:** Verifying that the software functions correctly according to requirements.
- **Non-functional Testing:** Assessing attributes such as performance, security, and usability.
- **System Testing:** Testing the complete and integrated software system.

8. **Exploratory Testing:** Exploratory testing is an unscripted approach where testers simultaneously learn about the software, design test cases, and execute tests. This approach is highly flexible and allows testers to quickly identify unexpected issues.

9. **Acceptance Testing:** Acceptance testing is conducted to ensure the software meets user requirements and is ready for deployment. It includes:

- **User Acceptance Testing (UAT):** Performed by end-users to validate the software meets their needs.

- **Operational Acceptance Testing (OAT):** Ensures the software is operationally ready, focusing on aspects like backup, recovery, and maintenance.

1.4. Essentials of Software Testing

Software testing is a multifaceted process that ensures the quality and reliability of software products. Understanding the essentials of software testing is crucial for effective test planning and execution. The following key elements are fundamental to successful software testing:

1. Test Planning and Documentation

- **Test Plan:** A comprehensive document outlining the testing strategy, objectives, resources, schedule, and scope. It defines the testing approach and helps manage the testing process.
- **Test Cases:** Detailed descriptions of individual tests, including input data, execution steps, and expected results. Test cases ensure systematic and repeatable testing.
- **Test Scripts:** In automated testing, these are scripts written to execute test cases using automation tools.

2. Test Environments

- **Development Environment:** Used by developers to write and initially test code.
- **Testing/Staging Environment:** A controlled environment that mirrors the production setup, used for thorough testing before release.
- **Production Environment:** The live environment where the software is deployed and used by end-users.

3. Types of Testing

- **Functional Testing:** Verifies that the software functions according to requirements. Includes unit, integration, system, and acceptance testing.
- **Non-functional Testing:** Assesses attributes like performance, security, usability, and reliability.
- **Regression Testing:** Ensures new changes do not introduce new defects or affect existing functionality.

4. Testing Techniques

- **Black Box Testing:** Focuses on input and output without considering internal code structure.
- **White Box Testing:** Involves testing internal code structure, logic, and implementation.

- **Grey Box Testing:** Combines both black box and white box testing techniques.

5. Test Automation

- **Automated Testing Tools:** Software like Selenium, JUnit, and TestNG that automate repetitive and regression tests.
- **CI/CD Integration:** Continuous Integration/Continuous Deployment pipelines integrate automated tests to ensure code changes are tested continuously and deployed seamlessly.

6. Defect Management

- **Bug Reporting:** Documenting identified defects with details such as steps to reproduce, severity, and screenshots.
- **Bug Tracking Tools:** Software like JIRA, Bugzilla, and Mantis that help manage and track the lifecycle of defects from identification to resolution.

7. Performance and Security Testing

- **Performance Testing:** Ensures the software performs well under expected load conditions. Includes load testing, stress testing, and scalability testing.
- **Security Testing:** Identifies vulnerabilities and ensures the software is secure against threats. Includes penetration testing and vulnerability scanning.

8. User Acceptance Testing (UAT)

- End-User Testing: Performed by actual users to validate the software meets their needs and requirements.
- Feedback Integration: Collecting and incorporating user feedback to improve the software before final release.

9. Test Metrics and Reporting

- **Test Coverage:** Measures the extent to which the software has been tested. Ensures all critical paths and functionalities are covered.
- **Defect Density:** Calculates the number of defects found per unit size of the software, helping assess quality.
- **Test Reports:** Summarize test activities, results, and metrics, providing stakeholders with insights into the quality and readiness of the software.

10. Continuous Improvement

- **Retrospectives:** Regular meetings to discuss what went well, what didn't, and how testing processes can be improved.
- **Process Optimization:** Implementing lessons learned and best practices to continuously enhance the efficiency and effectiveness of software testing.

1.5. Important Features of the Testing Process

The software testing process is integral to the software development lifecycle, ensuring the delivery of high-quality, reliable software products. Here are the important features that characterize an effective testing process:

1. Clear Objectives and Scope

- **Defined Goals:** Establish clear objectives for what the testing process aims to achieve, such as identifying defects, validating functionality, and assessing performance.
- **Scope Definition:** Clearly outline the scope of testing, including what will be tested and what is out of scope. This helps in focusing efforts and resources effectively.

2. Comprehensive Test Planning

- **Test Plan:** Develop a detailed test plan that includes the testing strategy, schedule, resources, test environment, and risk management plan. The test plan serves as a roadmap for the testing process.
- **Test Design:** Create detailed test cases and scenarios based on requirements and specifications. Test design should cover positive and negative test cases, edge cases, and user scenarios.

3. Test Environment Setup

- **Realistic Test Environment:** Set up a test environment that closely mimics the production environment. This includes hardware, software, network configurations, and databases.
- **Data Preparation:** Ensure test data is comprehensive and representative of real-world scenarios. This includes preparing various data sets for functional and performance testing.

4. Test Execution:

- **Manual Testing:** Execute test cases manually to identify defects and ensure the software behaves as expected.
- **Automated Testing:** Use automated testing tools to execute repetitive and regression tests, increasing efficiency and coverage.
- **Continuous Testing:** Integrate testing into the CI/CD pipeline to ensure continuous testing throughout the development process.

5. Defect Management:

- **Defect Tracking:** Use defect tracking tools to log, track, and manage defects. This includes assigning severity and priority levels to defects.

- **Defect Lifecycle Management:** Ensure a structured process for defect identification, reporting, analysis, fixing, retesting, and closure.

6. Performance and Security Testing:

- **Performance Testing:** Assess the software's performance under various conditions, including load testing, stress testing, and scalability testing.
- **Security Testing:** Identify and mitigate security vulnerabilities, ensuring the software is secure against potential threats.

7. User Acceptance Testing (UAT):

- **End-User Involvement:** Involve end-users in testing to validate that the software meets their needs and expectations.
- **Feedback Integration:** Collect and integrate feedback from UAT to improve the software before final release.

8. Test Metrics and Reporting:

- **Test Metrics:** Collect and analyze metrics such as test coverage, defect density, test execution rate, and defect resolution time.
- **Test Reporting:** Generate comprehensive test reports that provide insights into the testing process, including test results, defect status, and quality indicators. Share these reports with stakeholders for informed decision-making.

9. Continuous Improvement

- **Retrospectives:** Conduct regular retrospectives to review the testing process, identify areas for improvement, and implement best practices.
- **Process Optimization:** Continuously refine and optimize the testing process based on feedback and lessons learned.

10. Documentation

- Comprehensive Documentation: Maintain detailed documentation of test plans, test cases, test scripts, and test results. Documentation ensures repeatability and serves as a reference for future testing efforts.

11. Collaboration and Communication

- Cross-Functional Collaboration: Foster collaboration between testers, developers, business analysts, and other stakeholders to ensure a thorough understanding of requirements and effective issue resolution.
- Effective Communication: Maintain clear and open communication channels to ensure timely updates on test progress, defects, and overall software quality.

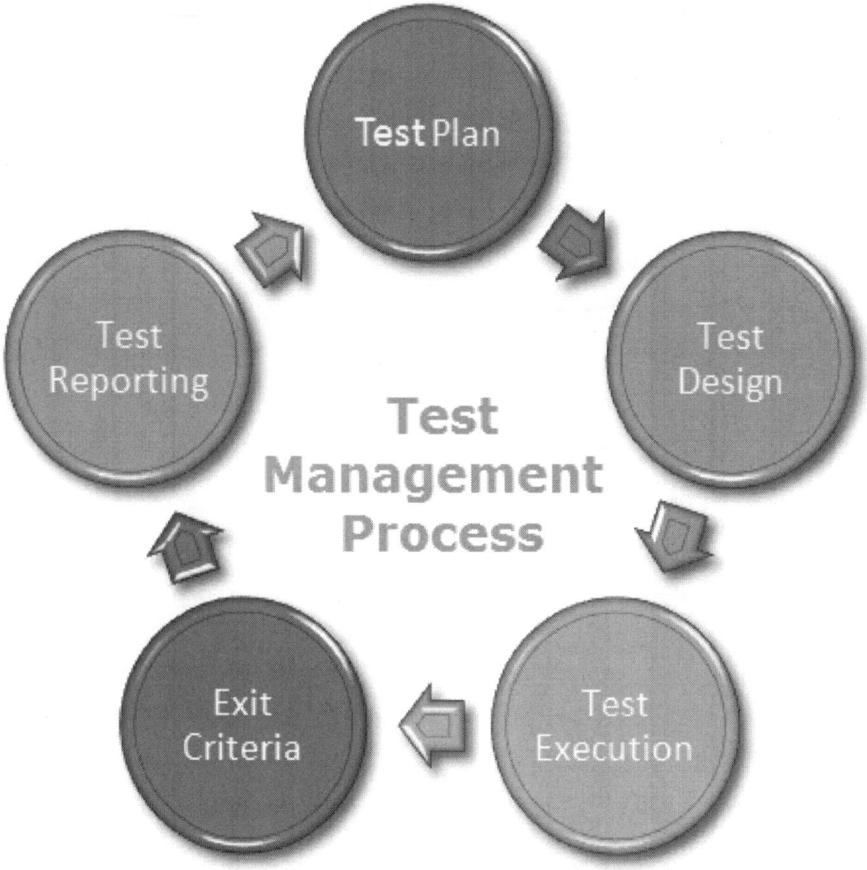

Fig 1: Important Features of testing process

1.6. Principles of Software Testing

Effective software testing is guided by a set of fundamental principles that ensure a structured and efficient approach to identifying defects and ensuring software quality. Here are the key principles of software testing:

1. Testing Shows the Presence of Defects

- **Defect Detection:** The primary goal of testing is to uncover defects in the software. It can show that defects are present, but it cannot prove that there are no defects.
- **Continuous Improvement:** Even if no defects are found, it does not imply the software is defect-free. Continuous testing and improvement are necessary.

2. Exhaustive Testing is Impossible

- **Limited Scope:** Testing everything (all combinations of inputs and preconditions) is impractical due to time and resource constraints.
- **Risk-Based Testing:** Focus on prioritizing tests based on risk and impact, ensuring critical areas are tested thoroughly.

3. Early Testing

- **Early Start:** Begin testing activities as early as possible in the software development lifecycle. Early testing helps in identifying defects early, reducing the cost and effort required for fixing them.
- **Shift Left:** Incorporate testing activities in the initial stages of development (requirement and design phases) to catch defects early.

4. Defect Clustering

- **Concentration of Defects:** A small number of modules typically contain most of the defects discovered during testing.
- **Focused Testing:** Focus testing efforts on these critical and defect-prone areas to maximize defect detection.

5. Pesticide Paradox

- **Test Case Effectiveness:** Repeated use of the same test cases will eventually find no new defects.
- **Test Case Review:** Regularly review and revise test cases, adding new ones to cover different aspects of the software and uncover new defects.

6. Testing is Context-Dependent

- **Tailored Approach:** The testing approach depends on the context of the software being tested, such as its purpose, complexity, and user base.
- **Contextual Adaptation:** Adapt the testing strategy to the specific needs of the project, using different techniques and tools as appropriate.

7. Absence-of-Errors Fallacy

- **Functionality vs. Usefulness:** Just because a software application is free of defects does not mean it is useful and meets user needs.
- **Requirement Validation:** Ensure that the software not only works correctly but also fulfills the specified requirements and provides value to the users.

8. The Principle of Pareto (80/20 Rule)

- **Defect Distribution:** Approximately 80% of problems are found in 20% of the modules.

- **Prioritization:** Prioritize testing efforts on the most critical and frequently used parts of the application to identify and fix the most impactful defects.

9. **Human Factor**

- **Collaboration:** Testing is a human process, and effective collaboration and communication among team members are crucial.
- **Bias Avoidance:** Testers should be aware of their biases and strive to maintain an objective and critical perspective during testing.

10. **Continuous Feedback**

- **Iterative Improvement:** Incorporate feedback from testing into the development process to continuously improve the software.
- **Feedback Loops:** Establish feedback loops between testers, developers, and other stakeholders to ensure issues are addressed promptly and effectively.

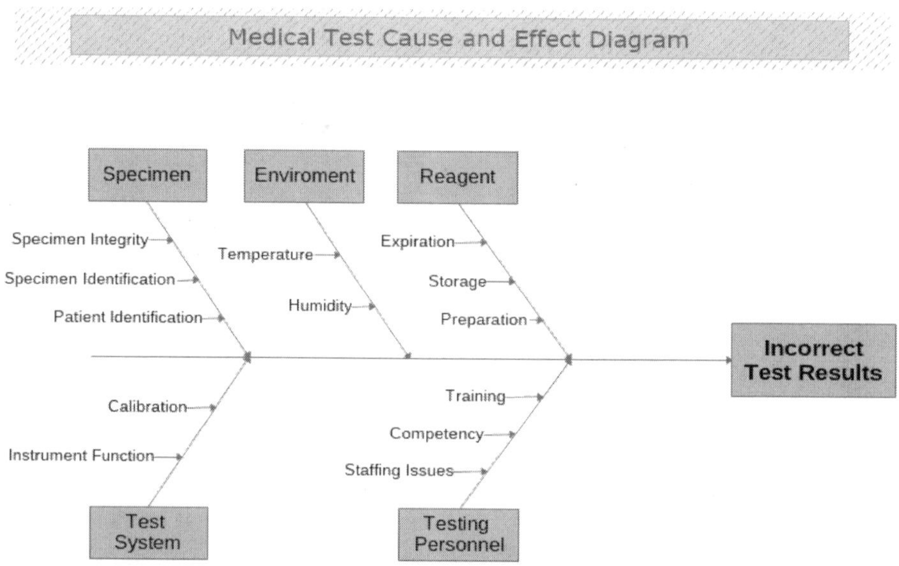

Fig 2: Test competency cause-effect diagram.

1.7.Salient Features of Good Testing

Good testing practices are essential for ensuring software quality and reliability. Here are the salient features that characterize effective testing:

1. Thorough Test Planning

- **Comprehensive Test Plan:** A well-documented test plan outlining the testing strategy, scope, objectives, resources, schedule, and risk management approach.
- **Clear Objectives:** Defining clear and achievable testing goals aligned with the overall project objectives.

2. Detailed Test Design and Coverage

- **Test Case Design:** Creating detailed and well-structured test cases that cover all functional and non-functional requirements.
- **Comprehensive Coverage:** Ensuring all critical paths, edge cases, and user scenarios are covered in the test cases.

3. Effective Use of Testing Techniques

- **Variety of Techniques:** Employing a mix of black box, white box, and grey box testing techniques to uncover different types of defects.
- **Context-Driven Testing:** Adapting testing techniques to the specific context and requirements of the software project.

4. Realistic Test Environment

- **Mirrored Environment:** Setting up a test environment that closely mimics the production environment, including hardware, software, network configurations, and databases.
- **Test Data:** Using realistic and comprehensive test data that represents actual usage scenarios.

5. Efficient Test Execution

- **Manual Testing:** Performing manual tests for exploratory, usability, and ad-hoc testing scenarios where human intuition is critical.
- **Automated Testing:** Leveraging automated testing tools for repetitive, regression, and performance testing to increase efficiency and coverage.
- **Continuous Testing:** Integrating testing into the CI/CD pipeline for continuous and iterative testing throughout the development lifecycle.

6. Defect Management and Reporting

- **Defect Tracking:** Using defect tracking tools to log, manage, and track the lifecycle of defects from identification to resolution.
- **Clear Reporting:** Providing clear, concise, and actionable defect reports with detailed steps to reproduce, severity, priority, and screenshots or logs.

7. Performance and Security Testing

- **Performance Testing:** Assessing the software's performance under various conditions, including load testing, stress testing, and scalability testing.
- **Security Testing:** Conducting thorough security assessments to identify vulnerabilities and ensure the software is secure against potential threats.

8. User Acceptance Testing (UAT)

- **Involvement of End-Users:** Engaging end-users in the testing process to validate that the software meets their needs and expectations.
- **Feedback Integration:** Collecting and incorporating feedback from UAT to improve the software before final release.

9. Test Metrics and Continuous Improvement

- **Test Metrics:** Collecting and analyzing test metrics such as test coverage, defect density, test execution rate, and defect resolution time.
- **Continuous Improvement:** Regularly reviewing testing processes and metrics to identify areas for improvement and implementing best practices.

10. Collaboration and Communication

- **Cross-Functional Collaboration:** Encouraging collaboration between testers, developers, business analysts, and other stakeholders to ensure a thorough understanding of requirements and effective issue resolution.
- **Effective Communication:** Maintaining clear and open communication channels to keep all stakeholders informed about test progress, defects, and overall software quality.

11. Documentation

- **Comprehensive Documentation:** Maintaining detailed documentation of test plans, test cases, test scripts, and test results to ensure repeatability and serve as a reference for future testing efforts.
- **Accessible Documentation:** Ensuring that all documentation is easily accessible to all team members and stakeholders.

12. Adaptability and Flexibility

- **Responsive to Change:** Being adaptable and flexible to changes in requirements, scope, or project timelines, and adjusting the testing approach accordingly.
- **Agile Testing:** Embracing agile methodologies to integrate testing seamlessly into the iterative development process.

1.8.Challenges in Software Testing

Software testing is a critical phase in the software development lifecycle, but it comes with various challenges. Addressing these challenges is essential to ensure effective and efficient testing. Here are some common challenges faced in software testing:

1. Time Constraints

- **Tight Deadlines:** Limited time available for thorough testing due to project schedules and release deadlines.
- **Balancing Act:** Striking a balance between comprehensive testing and timely delivery of the software.

2. Incomplete Requirements

- **Unclear Requirements:** Ambiguous, incomplete, or changing requirements make it difficult to design accurate test cases.
- **Scope Creep:** Late changes or additions to requirements can disrupt the testing process and extend timelines.

3. Insufficient Resources

- **Limited Budget:** Constraints on budget can limit the availability of tools, environments, and skilled testers.
- **Lack of Skilled Personnel:** Shortage of experienced testers with the necessary expertise to handle complex testing scenarios.

4. Complexity of Test Environments

- **Environment Setup:** Setting up and maintaining test environments that closely mimic production environments can be challenging and time-consuming.
- **Configuration Management:** Managing different configurations and ensuring consistency across various environments.

5. Evolving Technology

- **New Technologies:** Rapid advancements in technology and frequent updates to tools and platforms require continuous learning and adaptation.
- **Integration Testing:** Ensuring compatibility and seamless integration with other systems and platforms.

6. Data Management

- **Test Data Preparation:** Creating and managing realistic test data that covers all possible scenarios.
- **Data Privacy:** Ensuring compliance with data protection regulations and safeguarding sensitive data during testing.

7. Automation Challenges

- **Initial Setup:** High initial investment in time and resources to set up automation frameworks and scripts.
- **Maintenance:** Continuous maintenance and updating of automated test scripts to keep pace with changes in the software.

8. Defect Management

- **Defect Prioritization:** Effectively prioritizing defects based on severity, impact, and risk to ensure critical issues are addressed first.
- **Communication:** Ensuring clear and effective communication between testers, developers, and other stakeholders to resolve defects promptly.

9. Performance Testing

- **Realistic Load Simulation:** Accurately simulating real-world load conditions and user behavior to test performance under various scenarios.
- **Resource Intensive:** Performance testing can be resource-intensive, requiring significant computational power and specialized tools.

10. Security Testing

- **Identifying Vulnerabilities:** Ensuring thorough security testing to identify all potential vulnerabilities.
- **Keeping Up with Threats:** Staying updated with the latest security threats and testing for new vulnerabilities.

11. Regression Testing

- **Regression Test Coverage:** Ensuring that changes do not introduce new defects, which requires extensive and repeated testing.
- **Effort and Time:** Regression testing can be time-consuming, especially as the application grows and evolves.

12. User Acceptance Testing (UAT)

- **User Involvement:** Ensuring active and timely participation of end-users in the testing process.
- **Feedback Management:** Collecting, managing, and integrating feedback from users effectively.

13. Test Metrics and Reporting

- **Measuring Effectiveness:** Defining and collecting meaningful metrics that accurately reflect the effectiveness of testing efforts.
- **Clear Reporting:** Presenting test results and metrics in a clear, concise, and actionable manner for stakeholders.

14. Continuous Integration and Delivery (CI/CD)

- **Integration:** Integrating testing seamlessly into the CI/CD pipeline to ensure continuous and automated testing.
- **Consistency:** Ensuring consistent and reliable test results across various stages of the CI/CD pipeline.

15. Adapting to Agile and DevOps

- **Agile Testing:** Adapting traditional testing practices to fit into agile methodologies, requiring more collaboration and faster cycles.
- **DevOps Practices:** Integrating testing into DevOps practices to ensure continuous testing and faster delivery cycles.

1.9. Test Team Approach

A structured and collaborative approach within the test team is essential for ensuring effective and efficient software testing. Here are the key components of a test team approach:

1. Clear Roles and Responsibilities:

- **Test Manager/Lead:** Oversees the entire testing process, including planning, resource allocation, and reporting. Ensures that the team meets testing goals and objectives.
- **Test Engineers/Analysts:** Design and execute test cases, report defects, and ensure comprehensive test coverage. Specialized roles may include functional testers, automation testers, performance testers, and security testers.
- **Test Automation Engineers:** Develop and maintain automated test scripts and frameworks to support regression and continuous testing.
- **Performance Testers:** Focus on assessing the performance, scalability, and reliability of the software under different conditions.
- **Security Testers:** Conduct security assessments to identify vulnerabilities and ensure the software is secure.
- **UAT Coordinators:** Facilitate user acceptance testing, involving end-users to validate the software against business requirements.

2. Collaborative Planning and Strategy:

- **Test Strategy:** Develop a comprehensive test strategy that outlines the approach, scope, objectives, resources, and timelines. This strategy should align with the overall project goals.
- **Test Plan:** Create detailed test plans that include test objectives, test criteria, resources, schedules, and risk management. Regularly review and update the plan as needed.

3. Effective Communication:

- **Regular Meetings:** Hold regular team meetings to discuss progress, challenges, and next steps. This includes daily stand-ups, sprint planning, and retrospectives in agile environments.
- **Status Reporting:** Provide regular status reports to stakeholders, highlighting test progress, defects, risks, and any issues that need attention.
- **Collaboration Tools:** Utilize collaboration tools (e.g., JIRA, Confluence, Slack) to facilitate communication and collaboration among team members and other stakeholders.

4. Comprehensive Test Design:

- **Requirement Analysis:** Thoroughly analyze requirements to identify test conditions and design test cases that cover functional and non-functional aspects.
- **Test Case Development:** Create detailed test cases with clear steps, expected results, and test data. Review and validate test cases with stakeholders to ensure accuracy and completeness.

5. Test Environment Management:

- **Setup and Maintenance:** Ensure the test environment is set up correctly and mirrors the production environment as closely as possible. Regularly maintain and update the environment.
- **Data Management:** Prepare and manage test data that accurately represents real-world scenarios. Ensure data privacy and compliance with regulations.

6. Test Execution and Monitoring:

- **Manual Testing:** Execute test cases manually for scenarios that require human judgment, such as exploratory and usability testing.
- **Automated Testing:** Implement automated testing for regression, performance, and repetitive tasks to increase efficiency and coverage.
- **Continuous Testing:** Integrate testing into the CI/CD pipeline to ensure continuous testing throughout the development lifecycle.

7. Defect Management:

- **Defect Reporting:** Log defects with detailed information, including steps to reproduce, severity, priority, and screenshots or logs.
- **Defect Triage:** Regularly review and prioritize defects based on their impact and urgency. Ensure timely resolution and retesting of fixed defects.
- **Tracking Tools:** Use defect tracking tools (e.g., JIRA, Bugzilla) to manage and track defects throughout their lifecycle.

8. Performance and Security Testing:

- **Performance Testing:** Conduct performance tests to assess the software's behavior under various load conditions. Identify and address performance bottlenecks.
- **Security Testing:** Perform security assessments to identify vulnerabilities and ensure the software is secure against potential threats.

9. User Acceptance Testing (UAT):

- **End-User Involvement:** Engage end-users in the testing process to validate the software against business requirements and ensure it meets user needs.
- **Feedback Integration:** Collect and incorporate feedback from UAT to make necessary improvements before the final release.

10. Metrics and Continuous Improvement:

- **Test Metrics:** Collect and analyze metrics such as test coverage, defect density, test execution rate, and defect resolution time. Use these metrics to assess the effectiveness of the testing process.
- **Continuous Improvement:** Regularly review testing practices and processes to identify areas for improvement. Implement best practices and lessons learned to enhance the testing process.

11. Training and Development:

- **Skill Enhancement:** Provide ongoing training and development opportunities for the test team to stay updated with the latest tools, technologies, and best practices.
- **Knowledge Sharing:** Encourage knowledge sharing and collaboration within the team to leverage collective expertise and experience.

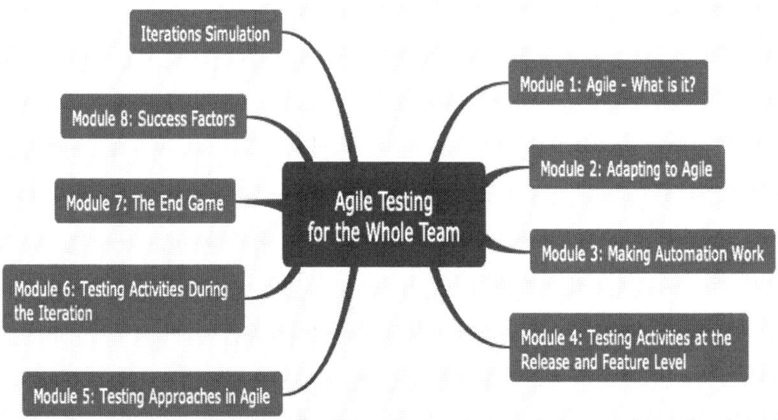

Fig 3: Test Team Approach diagram.

1.10. Cost of Testing

The cost of testing in software development is influenced by various factors and can be categorized into different types of costs. Understanding these costs helps in budgeting, resource allocation, and optimizing the testing process to achieve high-quality outcomes. Here's an overview of the key components that contribute to the cost of testing:

1. Personnel Costs:

- **Salaries:** The salaries of the testing team, including test managers, test engineers, automation engineers, performance testers, and security testers.
- **Training and Development:** Costs associated with training testers on new tools, technologies, and methodologies.
- **Consultants and Contractors:** Hiring external experts or consultants for specialized testing tasks.

2. Tool and Infrastructure Costs:

- **Testing Tools:** Purchasing or licensing fees for test management tools, automation tools, performance testing tools, and security testing tools.
- **Hardware and Software:** Costs of hardware and software needed to set up and maintain test environments that mimic the production environment.
- **Cloud Services:** Costs associated with using cloud services for testing environments and data storage.

3. Test Environment Setup:

- **Environment Configuration:** Setting up and configuring test environments to ensure they accurately reflect the production environment.
- **Maintenance:** Ongoing maintenance and updates of test environments to keep them in sync with production changes.
- **Data Preparation:** Creating and managing test data that accurately represents real-world scenarios.

4. Test Planning and Design:

- Requirement Analysis: Effort and time spent in understanding and analyzing requirements to design comprehensive test cases.
- Test Case Development: Creating detailed test cases and test scripts, including positive and negative scenarios.

5. Test Execution:

- **Manual Testing:** Time and effort spent on executing test cases manually, particularly for exploratory, usability, and ad-hoc testing.

- **Automated Testing:** Initial setup costs for automation frameworks and ongoing costs for maintaining and updating automated test scripts.
- **Regression Testing:** Continuous execution of regression tests to ensure new changes do not introduce defects.

6. Defect Management:

- **Defect Reporting:** Time and effort involved in identifying, logging, and reporting defects.
- **Defect Triage and Retesting:** Costs associated with prioritizing, fixing, and retesting defects to ensure they are resolved correctly.

7. Performance and Security Testing:

- **Performance Testing:** Costs related to performance testing, including tools, infrastructure, and the effort required to simulate real-world load conditions.
- **Security Testing:** Expenses associated with conducting security assessments, penetration testing, and vulnerability scanning.

8. User Acceptance Testing (UAT):

- **End-User Involvement:** Costs of involving end-users in the testing process, including coordination, feedback collection, and integration of feedback.
- **Logistics:** Expenses related to setting up UAT environments and supporting end-users during testing.

9. Reporting and Metrics:

- **Test Reporting:** Time and effort required to generate comprehensive test reports, including test results, defect status, and quality metrics.
- **Metrics Analysis:** Analyzing test metrics to assess the effectiveness of the testing process and identify areas for improvement.

10. Continuous Improvement:

- **Process Optimization:** Costs associated with reviewing and improving testing processes based on lessons learned and best practices.
- **Retrospectives:** Conducting regular retrospectives to identify and implement process improvements.

11. Opportunity Costs:

- **Delayed Release:** Potential revenue loss due to delayed release if testing takes longer than planned.
- **Quality Issues:** Costs related to poor quality if testing is insufficient, including customer dissatisfaction, support costs, and brand damage.

1.11. Categories of Defects

Defects in software can be categorized based on various criteria such as their nature, severity, and origin. Identifying and categorizing defects helps in prioritizing their resolution and understanding the areas of the software that need improvement. Here are the main categories of defects:

1. Functional Defects:

- **Missing Functionality:** Features or functions that are missing from the software, which were specified in the requirements.
- **Incorrect Functionality:** Features or functions that do not work as intended or as specified in the requirements.
- **Extra Functionality:** Unintended features or functions that were not specified in the requirements but are present in the software.

2. Performance Defects:

- **Slow Performance:** The software does not meet performance requirements, such as response time, throughput, or load handling.
- **Resource Usage:** The software consumes more resources (CPU, memory, bandwidth) than expected or specified, leading to performance degradation.

3. Usability Defects:

- **User Interface Issues:** Problems with the user interface that make the software difficult to use, such as unclear navigation, inconsistent layout, or poor design.
- **Accessibility Issues:** The software does not comply with accessibility standards, making it difficult for users with disabilities to use.

4. Compatibility Defects:

- **Platform Compatibility:** Issues that arise when the software does not function correctly across different platforms (e.g., operating systems, browsers, devices).
- **Backward Compatibility:** The software does not work with older versions of the system or data formats.

5. Security Defects:

Vulnerabilities: Weaknesses that can be exploited by attackers to gain unauthorized access or cause harm, such as SQL injection, cross-site scripting (XSS), or buffer overflow.

- **Data Privacy Issues:** Failures to protect sensitive data, leading to potential breaches of privacy regulations.

6. Data Defects:

- **Data Integrity:** Issues where the data is corrupted, inconsistent, or incorrect.
- **Data Validation:** Defects related to improper validation of input data, leading to invalid or harmful data being processed.

7. Logic Defects:

- **Algorithm Errors:** Flaws in the logic or algorithms used in the software, leading to incorrect results or behavior.
- **Calculation Errors:** Mistakes in arithmetic operations or formulae leading to incorrect calculations.

8. Boundary Defects:

- **Boundary Value Issues:** Errors that occur when the software does not handle boundary conditions (e.g., minimum, maximum values) correctly.
- **Edge Case Failures:** Defects that appear only under specific and often rare conditions at the edges of the input or operational range.

9. Workflow Defects:

- **Process Flow Issues:** Problems in the sequence of operations or workflow within the software, leading to incorrect or unintended outcomes.
- **State Transition Errors:** Incorrect handling of state changes or transitions in stateful systems.

10. Documentation Defects:

- **Incorrect Documentation:** Errors in the software documentation, such as user manuals, help files, or API documentation, that mislead or confuse users.
- **Missing Documentation:** Lack of necessary documentation, making it difficult for users or developers to understand or use the software.

11. Environmental Defects:

- **Configuration Issues:** Problems arising from incorrect configuration settings or parameters in the deployment environment.
- **External System Interactions:** Issues with the integration or interaction between the software and external systems or services.

12. Regression Defects:

- **New Defects:** New issues introduced into the software after changes or updates, often due to code modifications or enhancements.
- **Reopened Defects:** Previously fixed defects that reappear after further changes or updates.

13. Interface Defects:

- API Issues: Problems with the application programming interfaces (APIs) that the software exposes or consumes.
- Interoperability Issues: Defects in the interaction between different modules, components, or systems.

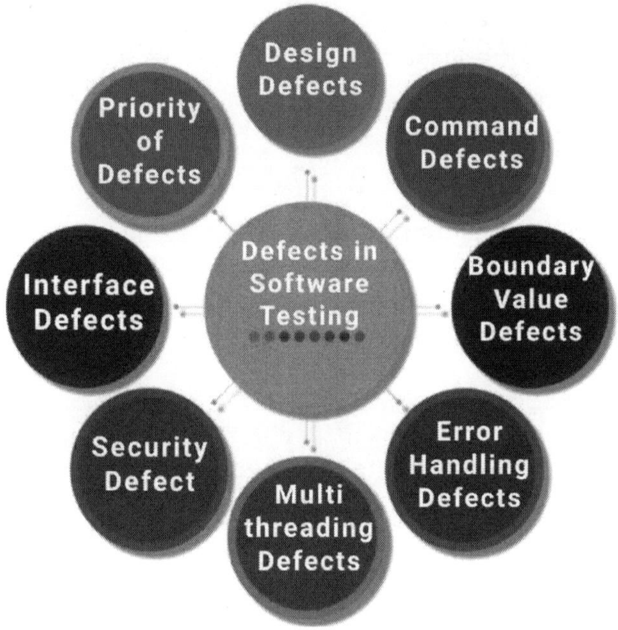

Fig 4: Categories of defect

1.12. Test Methodologies

Test methodologies are structured approaches and strategies used in software testing to ensure comprehensive test coverage and effective defect detection. These methodologies vary based on the project requirements, development model, and specific goals of the testing phase. Here are the key test methodologies commonly used:

1. Waterfall Methodology:

- **Sequential Approach:** Testing is conducted in a linear and sequential phase following requirements gathering, design, implementation, and testing.
- **Phase Completion:** Testing starts only after the development phase is completed.

- Documentation: Heavy emphasis on documentation, with detailed test plans and test cases created before execution.

2. V-Model (Validation and Verification Model):

- **Parallel Development and Testing:** Each development phase has a corresponding testing phase, ensuring validation and verification occur simultaneously.
- **Early Testing:** Testing activities are planned early in the lifecycle, parallel to development activities.
- **Validation and Verification:** Emphasizes both validation (are we building the right product?) and verification (are we building the product right?).

3. Agile Methodology:

- **Iterative and Incremental:** Testing is conducted iteratively in short cycles called sprints, allowing for continuous feedback and improvements.
- **Continuous Integration and Testing:** Frequent integration and testing of code to identify defects early and often.
- **Collaboration:** Emphasis on collaboration between developers, testers, and stakeholders, with regular stand-ups, reviews, and retrospectives.

4. Scrum Testing:

- **Sprint Cycles:** Testing is planned and executed within fixed-length iterations called sprints.
- **Product Backlog:** Test cases are derived from user stories in the product backlog.
- **Daily Stand-ups:** Regular communication among team members to discuss progress, challenges, and next steps.

5. Kanban Testing:

- **Visual Workflow Management:** Uses Kanban boards to visualize the workflow and manage testing tasks.
- **Continuous Delivery:** Focuses on continuous delivery and improvement without fixed-length iterations.
- **Work-in-Progress (WIP) Limits:** Limits on the number of tasks in progress to ensure manageable workload and focus on task completion.

6. Spiral Methodology:

- **Risk-Driven:** Combines iterative development with a risk-driven approach, focusing on risk assessment and mitigation.
- **Cyclical Phases:** Each cycle includes planning, risk analysis, engineering, and evaluation, with testing occurring throughout.

- **Prototyping:** Emphasizes early creation of prototypes to identify and mitigate risks early in the project.

7. DevOps Testing:

- **Continuous Testing:** Integrates testing into the DevOps pipeline, enabling continuous integration, continuous testing, and continuous delivery.
- **Automation:** Heavy reliance on test automation to ensure rapid feedback and reduce manual testing efforts.
- **Collaboration:** Close collaboration between development, operations, and testing teams to streamline processes and improve quality.

8. Behavior-Driven Development (BDD):

- **User Stories:** Test cases are written in natural language based on user stories, making them understandable to all stakeholders.
- **Given-When-Then Format:** Test scenarios follow the Given-When-Then format to describe preconditions, actions, and expected outcomes.
- **Collaboration:** Encourages collaboration between developers, testers, and business analysts to ensure a shared understanding of requirements.

9. Test-Driven Development (TDD):

- **Test First:** Writing test cases before writing the actual code.
- **Short Development Cycles:** Develop code in small increments, with each increment starting with a test.
- **Refactoring:** Continuous refactoring of code to improve quality and maintainability.

10. Exploratory Testing:

- **Simultaneous Learning:** Test design and test execution occur simultaneously, with testers exploring the software to find defects.
- **Experience-Based:** Relies on the tester's experience, intuition, and creativity to uncover issues that scripted tests might miss.
- **Adaptability:** Flexible and adaptable approach, allowing testers to respond to findings and adjust their focus as needed.

11. Risk-Based Testing:

- **Risk Assessment:** Identifying and prioritizing testing activities based on the potential risk and impact of defects.
- **Focus on Critical Areas:** Allocating more resources and effort to testing high-risk areas of the application.
- **Continuous Evaluation:** Ongoing assessment and adjustment of testing priorities based on changing risk profiles.

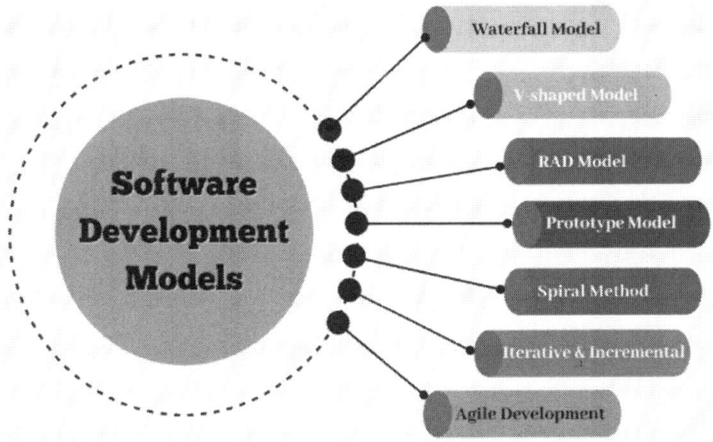

Fig 5: Software model diagram.

1.13. Skills Required by a Tester

Effective software testers possess a blend of technical, analytical, and interpersonal skills to ensure the quality and functionality of software applications. Here's an overview of the essential skills required by a tester:

1. Technical Skills:

- **Programming Knowledge:** Understanding of programming languages (e.g., Java, Python, C#) to create and maintain automated test scripts.
- **Database/SQL Knowledge:** Ability to write and execute SQL queries to validate data integrity and conduct backend testing.
- **Test Automation Tools:** Proficiency in using test automation tools such as Selenium, QTP, JUnit, TestNG, and LoadRunner.
- **Defect Tracking Tools:** Familiarity with defect tracking and test management tools like JIRA, Bugzilla, and TestRail.
- **CI/CD Tools:** Experience with continuous integration and continuous delivery tools like Jenkins, Bamboo, and GitLab.
- **Operating Systems:** Knowledge of different operating systems (Windows, Linux, macOS) to test software across various environments.
- **Scripting Languages:** Proficiency in scripting languages like JavaScript, VBScript, and Shell scripting for automation and environment setup.

2. Analytical Skills:

- **Attention to Detail:** Ability to spot even the smallest defects and inconsistencies in software applications.

- **Problem-Solving:** Strong problem-solving skills to identify the root cause of defects and suggest appropriate solutions.
- **Logical Thinking:** Logical and critical thinking to design effective test cases and scenarios.
- **Requirement Analysis:** Skills to thoroughly analyze and understand requirements, specifications, and user stories to create relevant test cases.

3. Testing Skills:

- **Manual Testing:** Expertise in executing test cases manually, including functional, regression, and exploratory testing.
- **Automation Testing:** Skills to develop and execute automated test scripts to improve testing efficiency and coverage.
- **Performance Testing:** Knowledge of performance testing techniques and tools to assess the software's performance under various conditions.
- **Security Testing:** Ability to conduct security testing to identify vulnerabilities and ensure software security.
- **Usability Testing:** Skills to evaluate the user-friendliness and accessibility of the software from an end-user perspective.
- **Mobile Testing:** Experience in testing mobile applications on different devices and platforms (iOS, Android).

4. Soft Skills:

- **Communication:** Strong written and verbal communication skills to effectively report defects, communicate with team members, and collaborate with stakeholders.
- **Collaboration:** Ability to work well in a team, including developers, business analysts, and other testers, to ensure project success.
- **Adaptability:** Flexibility to adapt to changing requirements, tools, and technologies in a dynamic testing environment.
- **Time Management:** Effective time management skills to prioritize tasks, manage workload, and meet deadlines.
- **Attention to Detail:** A meticulous approach to testing, ensuring thoroughness in identifying and documenting defects.

5. Domain Knowledge:

- **Industry Knowledge:** Understanding of the specific industry or domain (e.g., finance, healthcare, e-commerce) to create relevant test scenarios and cases.
- **Business Processes:** Knowledge of the business processes and workflows to ensure that the software meets business requirements and user needs.

6. Learning and Improvement:

- **Continuous Learning:** Willingness to keep up with new tools, technologies, and methodologies in the rapidly evolving field of software testing.
- **Feedback Integration:** Ability to receive and integrate feedback from peers, managers, and users to improve testing processes and outcomes.
- **Certification:** Pursuit of professional certifications (e.g., ISTQB, CSTE) to validate skills and knowledge in software testing.

UNIT 2

SOFTWARE TESTING ENVIRONMENT

2.0 Assessing Capabilities

Assessing capabilities involves evaluating the strengths, weaknesses, and potential of individuals, teams, organizations, or systems across various contexts such as business, technology, and project management. For individuals, this includes assessing skills, competencies, experience, knowledge, and learning agility, often through self-assessments, peer reviews, and performance metrics. Team capability assessment focuses on identifying skill gaps, collaboration, communication, productivity, and problem-solving abilities. At the organizational level, it's crucial to ensure strategic alignment, process efficiency, technology adequacy, workforce capability, and financial health. Project capability assessment involves evaluating project management skills, resource availability, risk management, and the ability to deliver expected outcomes. Technological capabilities are assessed by examining infrastructure readiness, innovation potential, system integration, and cybersecurity measures.

Several methods and tools, such as SWOT analysis, benchmarking, surveys, performance metrics, and Capability Maturity Models (CMM), are used to conduct these assessments. Developing capabilities involves implementing training and development programs, process improvements, technology upgrades, and change management initiatives. Continuous improvement and monitoring are essential, achieved through regular reviews, KPI tracking, and feedback loops to ensure ongoing capability development. Case studies, such as evaluating a startup's ability to scale operations or a team's readiness to adopt Agile methodologies, provide practical examples of capability assessment in action. The assessment process concludes with a summary of findings, an action plan to address gaps and build on strengths, and a discussion on how continuous capability assessment supports long-term success.

2.1 Staff Competency

In a software testing environment, staff competency is crucial for ensuring the quality and reliability of software products. Competency in this context refers to the combination of technical skills, testing methodologies, experience, and behaviour's that software testers need to perform their roles effectively, contributing to the overall success of the testing process and the final product.

Key Aspects of Staff Competency in Software Testing

1. Core Competencies: These are the fundamental skills that all software testers should possess, regardless of their specific focus areas. Core competencies include a strong understanding of software development life cycles (SDLC), familiarity with different types of testing (such as functional, non-functional, manual, and automated testing), and the ability to use various testing tools and platforms effectively. Additionally, testers must have strong analytical skills to identify defects, good communication skills for reporting issues clearly, and a commitment to continuous learning to stay updated with the latest testing trends and tools.

2. Role-Specific Competencies: In the software testing environment, different roles may require specific competencies. For example, an automation tester needs to be proficient in scripting languages and familiar with automation frameworks like Selenium or TestNG. A performance tester should be skilled in using performance testing tools such as JMeter or LoadRunner and have a deep 444testing tools like OWASP ZAP or Burp Suite and knowledge of common security vulnerabilities.

3. Behavioural Competencies: Behavioural competencies are critical in the software testing environment, as they influence how testers interact with other team members and handle challenges. Important behavioural competencies include attention to detail, adaptability to changing requirements, perseverance in finding hard-to-detect bugs, and collaboration skills to work effectively with developers, project managers, and other stakeholders. Ethical judgment is also vital, particularly in handling sensitive data during testing.

4. Professional Development: The software testing landscape is constantly evolving, with new tools, technologies, and methodologies emerging regularly. Therefore, ongoing professional development is essential for maintaining and enhancing staff competency. This can be achieved through training programs, certifications like ISTQB (International Software Testing Qualifications Board), attending industry conferences, and engaging in continuous learning opportunities. Regular knowledge sharing within the team, such as through workshops or peer reviews, also contributes to professional growth.

5. Competency Assessments: Regular competency assessments are crucial in a software testing environment to identify strengths and areas for improvement. These assessments can be conducted through technical tests, peer reviews, and performance evaluations by managers. Testers might also be evaluated based on the quality and efficiency of their test cases, defect identification rates, and the effectiveness of their communication with other team members. The insights gained from these assessments help in creating targeted development plans for individual testers and aligning their skills with the needs of the project.

6. Competency Frameworks: Many software testing teams use competency frameworks to define the specific skills and behaviours required for different testing roles. These frameworks provide clear guidelines for recruitment, performance management, and career development. For example, a framework might outline the progression path from a junior manual tester to a senior automation engineer, detailing the competencies required at each level.

7. Impact on Project Success: High staff competency in a software testing environment leads to more efficient testing processes, early detection of defects, and overall higher software quality. Competent testers can adapt to various testing challenges, contribute to smoother project execution, and help ensure that software products meet or exceed user expectations. This not only enhances customer satisfaction but also reduces the risk of costly post-release issues.

2.2. User Satisfaction-Creating an Environment Supportive of Software Testing

Creating an environment that supports software testing is essential for achieving high user satisfaction. This environment should foster collaboration, continuous learning, and the use of advanced tools and methodologies. By integrating testing into every phase of the software development life cycle, from planning to deployment, teams can ensure that issues are identified and addressed early, reducing the risk of defects in the final product. An effective testing environment also encourages open communication between testers, developers, and stakeholders, enabling quick resolution of any issues that arise. Access to the latest testing tools and technologies, along with opportunities for professional development, ensures that testers are well-equipped to handle complex testing scenarios. Moreover, fostering a culture of quality where testing is seen as a shared responsibility among all team members helps in creating a robust and reliable software product. When these elements are in place, the likelihood of delivering a product that meets or exceeds user expectations increases significantly, leading to higher user satisfaction and stronger customer loyalty.

To further enhance user satisfaction through a supportive software testing environment, it's crucial to emphasize the importance of a well-defined testing strategy. This strategy should be aligned with the overall project goals and should clearly outline the types of testing to be conducted, the tools to be used, and the criteria for success. By establishing a comprehensive testing plan that includes functional, non-functional, performance, security, and usability testing, teams can ensure that every aspect of the software meets the desired quality standards.

Another key aspect of a supportive testing environment is the integration of automated testing. Automation helps to accelerate the testing process, allowing for more frequent testing cycles and quicker feedback on code changes. This is particularly important in Agile and DevOps environments, where continuous integration and continuous delivery (CI/CD) are the norms. Automated tests can be run repeatedly with minimal manual intervention, ensuring that new features and updates do not introduce regressions or other issues. This not only improves the efficiency of the testing process but also helps to maintain a high level of product quality over time.

Moreover, providing testers with a stable and well-configured testing environment is essential. This includes access to realistic test data, well-maintained test environments that mimic production settings, and reliable infrastructure that supports seamless testing activities. A stable environment minimizes the risk of false positives or negatives in test results, leading to more accurate assessments of the software's quality.

User satisfaction is also influenced by the responsiveness of the testing team to feedback. Establishing clear channels for reporting bugs and issues, along with a transparent process for tracking and resolving these issues, helps to build trust with end-users. When users see that their concerns are taken seriously and are addressed promptly, their confidence in the product and the development team increases.

Additionally, encouraging cross-functional collaboration is vital in creating a supportive testing environment. Testers, developers, product owners, and other stakeholders should work closely together throughout the development process. This collaboration ensures that everyone is aligned on the project's objectives and that potential issues are identified and mitigated early. When testers have a deep understanding of the user requirements and business goals, they can tailor their testing efforts to ensure that the software delivers real value to the end-users.

Finally, fostering a culture of continuous improvement within the testing environment can greatly contribute to user satisfaction. This involves regularly reviewing testing processes and outcomes to identify areas for improvement, adopting new tools and techniques as they become available, and encouraging testers to learn and grow in their roles. By staying ahead of industry trends and continuously refining testing practices, teams can consistently deliver high-quality software that meets or exceeds user expectations, leading to higher levels of user satisfaction and long-term success for the organization.

2.3 Building the Software Testing Process

Building a robust software testing process is crucial for delivering high-quality software that meets user expectations and performs reliably in real-world conditions. The process begins with defining clear testing objectives, which must align with user needs and business goals to ensure that the focus remains on delivering genuine value. Setting well-defined objectives helps in guiding the entire testing process and ensures that every aspect of the software is evaluated effectively.

Developing a comprehensive test strategy is the next step. This strategy should outline the various types of testing required, such as functional testing to validate that the software meets its requirements, non-functional testing to assess performance, usability, and security, and user acceptance testing (UAT) to ensure the software meets end-user needs. The strategy should also detail the selection of appropriate tools and technologies, such as test management software, automation frameworks, and performance monitoring tools. Additionally, it should define the scope of testing, specifying what will be tested and what will not, to ensure resources are effectively utilized.

A detailed test plan is essential for guiding the testing process. This plan should include the specific testing activities to be conducted, a schedule for testing, the resources needed, and the expected deliverables. It should outline the test cases, the environments in which tests will be executed, and the criteria for determining when testing is complete. Assigning roles and responsibilities clearly ensures that everyone involved understands their tasks, from test execution to defect management.

Designing test cases involves creating scenarios that cover all functional and non-functional requirements of the software, including edge cases and potential failure points. Each test case should include detailed steps, input data, and expected results. Prioritizing these test cases based on risk, impact, and criticality helps in focusing on the most important areas first, ensuring that critical functionalities are tested thoroughly.

Setting up a realistic test environment is crucial for accurate testing. This includes configuring hardware, software, and network settings to closely mimic the production environment and preparing test data that reflects real-world conditions. A stable and well-configured environment minimizes the risk of false positives or negatives in test results and ensures reliable outcomes.

The execution phase involves both manual and automated testing. Manual testing is important for scenarios that require human judgment, such as exploratory and usability testing, while automated testing is used for repetitive tasks like regression and performance testing. Automation enhances efficiency and coverage, particularly in continuous integration and continuous delivery (CI/CD) environments, where frequent testing is necessary.

Effective defect management is a key component of the testing process. Defects identified during testing should be logged promptly in a defect tracking system with detailed information to facilitate resolution. Defects should be prioritized based on their severity and impact on the software, with critical issues addressed immediately to prevent delays. Regression testing should be performed to ensure that fixes do not introduce new defects and that the software continues to function as expected.

Post-testing reviews are essential for continuous improvement. Analyzing test results, reviewing the effectiveness of test cases, and evaluating the efficiency of the testing process help identify areas for enhancement. Feedback from these reviews should be used to refine testing strategies, improve test coverage, and adopt new tools and techniques.

Final validation involves conducting User Acceptance Testing (UAT) to ensure the software meets user requirements and expectations. This phase often includes gathering feedback from end-users to verify that the software performs well in real-world scenarios. Obtaining formal sign-off from stakeholders confirms that the software is ready for release.

Comprehensive documentation is vital for maintaining a clear record of the testing process. This includes test plans, test cases, defect logs, and test reports. Proper documentation not only supports future maintenance and regression testing but also provides valuable insights for ongoing quality assurance efforts.

By establishing a structured testing process that includes defining clear objectives, developing a comprehensive strategy, designing detailed test cases, setting up realistic test environments, and leveraging both manual and automated testing, teams can ensure the delivery of high-quality software. Continuous improvement, effective defect management, and thorough documentation further contribute to a successful testing process, ultimately leading to greater user satisfaction and project success.

2.4. Testing Guidelines

Testing guidelines are essential for ensuring that software testing processes are effective, consistent, and aligned with best practices. They provide a framework for conducting tests systematically and help in achieving reliable and high-quality results. Here are comprehensive guidelines for software testing:

1. Establish Clear Objectives

Define Goals: Set specific, measurable objectives for the testing process, such as verifying that the software meets functional requirements, performs under expected load, or is free from critical defects.

Align with Requirements: Ensure that the testing objectives are aligned with user requirements and business goals to deliver a product that meets end-user needs.

2. Develop a Comprehensive Test Strategy

Identify Testing Types: Determine the types of testing required, such as functional, non-functional, performance, security, and usability testing, based on the nature of the software and project requirements.

Select Tools and Technologies: Choose appropriate testing tools and technologies that support the types of testing identified. This may include test management tools, automation frameworks, and performance monitoring tools.

Define Scope and Coverage: Clearly define the scope of testing, including what will be tested and what will not, to ensure that all critical aspects of the software are covered.

3. Create a Detailed Test Plan

Outline Testing Activities: Develop a test plan that outlines the specific testing activities, schedule, resources, and deliverables. Include details on test case development, execution procedures, and criteria for test completion.

Assign Roles and Responsibilities: Clearly define the roles and responsibilities of team members involved in the testing process to ensure accountability and efficient execution.

4. Design Effective Test Cases

Cover All Scenarios: Create detailed test cases that cover all functional and non-functional requirements, including edge cases and potential failure points. Each test case should include steps, input data, and expected results.

Prioritize Test Cases: Prioritize test cases based on risk, impact, and criticality to ensure that the most important functionalities are tested thoroughly.

5. Set Up a Realistic Test Environment

Configure Environment: Establish test environments that closely mimic the production environment, including hardware, software, and network configurations. This ensures that test results are accurate and reliable.

Prepare Test Data: Use realistic test data that reflects real-world conditions to ensure comprehensive testing of the software's functionality.

6. Execute Tests Systematically

Manual Testing: Conduct manual testing for scenarios requiring human judgment, such as exploratory and usability testing. Document findings and observations thoroughly.

Automated Testing: Implement automated testing for repetitive tasks like regression and performance testing. Ensure that automated tests are maintained and updated regularly.

7. Manage Defects Effectively

Log Defects Promptly: Record defects in a defect tracking system with detailed information to facilitate quick resolution. Include steps to reproduce, screenshots, and severity levels.

Prioritize and Assign: Prioritize defects based on severity and impact, and assign them to the appropriate developers for resolution. Address critical defects immediately to avoid delays.

8. Perform Regression Testing

Re-Test Fixed Issues: After defects are fixed, re-test the affected areas to ensure that the issues have been resolved. Perform regression testing to confirm that new changes do not introduce new defects.

Automate Regression Tests: Automate regression tests where possible to improve efficiency and reduce the risk of human error.

9. Review and Improve Testing Processes

Conduct Test Reviews: Regularly review test results, effectiveness of test cases, and the efficiency of the testing process. Use feedback from these reviews to identify areas for improvement.

Implement Continuous Improvement: Continuously refine testing strategies, adopt new tools and techniques and enhance test coverage based on review findings and industry trends.

10. Conduct Final Validation and Sign-Of

User Acceptance Testing (UAT): Perform UAT to verify that the software meets user requirements and expectations. Gather feedback from end-users to ensure the software performs well in real-world scenarios.

Obtain Formal Sign-Off: Secure formal sign-off from stakeholders to confirm that the software is ready for release. This ensures that all critical issues have been addressed and the product is fit for deployment.

11. Document and Report

Create Comprehensive Reports: Document the testing process, including test cases, defect logs, test results, and any deviations from the original plan. Provide detailed reports to stakeholders summarizing the overall quality of the software.

Maintain Test Artifacts: Store all test artifacts for future reference, including test plans, test cases, and defect logs. These documents are valuable for future maintenance and regression testing.

12. Ensure Compliance and Security

Adhere to Standards: Follow industry standards and best practices for software testing to ensure compliance and maintain quality. This includes adhering to standards like ISO/IEC/IEEE 29119 for software testing.Consider Security: Integrate security testing into the overall testing strategy to identify and address potential vulnerabilities. Ensure that the software is secure and compliant with relevant regulations and standards.

By adhering to these guidelines, teams can build a structured and effective software testing process that enhances the quality of the software, reduces the risk of defects, and improves user satisfaction. A well-executed testing process contributes to successful project delivery and long-term product reliability. Certainly! Here are additional points to further enhance the software testing guidelines:

13. Emphasize Test Planning and Preparation

Define Test Objectives: Clearly articulate the objectives of each test phase to ensure alignment with overall project goals.

Develop Test Scenarios: Create comprehensive test scenarios that capture various user journeys and system interactions to cover all possible use cases.

Plan for Test Data Management: Develop a strategy for creating, maintaining, and refreshing test data to ensure it remains relevant and accurate.

14. Focus on Test Coverage and Traceability

Ensure Comprehensive Coverage: Verify that test cases cover all aspects of the software, including all requirements, user stories, and potential risks. Utilize traceability matrices to map test cases to requirements.

Address Gaps in Coverage: Regularly review test coverage and address any gaps by adding new test cases or adjusting existing ones to ensure complete validation of the software.

15. Implement Risk-Based Testing

Identify Risks: Assess potential risks associated with the software, such as high-impact functionalities or critical business processes.

Prioritize Testing: Focus testing efforts on high-risk areas to ensure that critical components are thoroughly evaluated and that potential issues are identified early.

16. Integrate Testing with Development

Adopt Agile Testing Practices: In Agile environments, integrate testing into the development process with practices such as Test-Driven Development (TDD) and Behaviour-Driven Development (BDD).

Collaborate with Developers: Foster collaboration between testers and developers to ensure that testing is aligned with development efforts and that feedback is communicated effectively.

17. Monitor and Measure Testing Effectiveness

Track Key Metrics: Monitor key performance indicators (KPIs) such as defect density, test case execution rate, and test coverage to evaluate the effectiveness of the testing process.

Analyze Test Results: Analyze test results to identify patterns and trends, and use this data to make informed decisions about the quality of the software and the effectiveness of testing efforts.

18. Address Environment and Configuration Management

Manage Test Environments: Ensure that test environments are properly configured, maintained, and isolated from production environments to avoid contamination and ensure accurate results.

Handle Configuration Changes: Implement configuration management practices to track and manage changes to the test environment, ensuring that any updates or modifications are properly documented and controlled.

19. Enhance Test Automation Strategies

Identify Automation Opportunities: Determine which test cases and processes are best suited for automation based on factors such as frequency, complexity, and stability.

Maintain Automation Scripts: Regularly update and maintain automated test scripts to ensure they remain relevant and effective as the software evolves.

20. Focus on Usability and User Experience

Conduct Usability Testing: Perform usability testing to evaluate the software's ease of use, accessibility, and overall user experience.

Gather User Feedback: Collect feedback from end-users to identify areas for improvement and ensure that the software meets user expectations and provides a positive experience.

21. Plan for Performance and Scalability Testing

Assess Performance: Conduct performance testing to evaluate the software's responsiveness, stability, and resource utilization under different conditions and loads.

Test for Scalability: Verify that the software can scale effectively to handle increasing volumes of data or user interactions without performance degradation.

22. Implement Security Testing Practices

Conduct Vulnerability Assessments: Perform security testing to identify vulnerabilities and weaknesses in the software that could be exploited by malicious actors.

Ensure Compliance: Ensure that the software meets relevant security standards and regulations, such as GDPR, HIPAA, or PCI-DSS, to protect sensitive data and maintain compliance.

23. Incorporate Continuous Integration and Continuous Delivery (CI/CD)

Integrate Testing in CI/CD Pipelines: Incorporate automated testing into CI/CD pipelines to enable continuous validation of code changes and ensure that software is tested with each build and deployment.

Monitor Build and Release Metrics: Track metrics related to builds and releases to identify and address any issues that arise during the CI/CD process.

24. Ensure Documentation and Knowledge Sharing

Document Test Processes: Maintain comprehensive documentation of testing processes, methodologies, and best practices to ensure consistency and facilitate knowledge sharing within the team.

Share Knowledge: Promote knowledge sharing through regular team meetings, workshops, and training sessions to keep the team informed about new tools, techniques, and industry trends.

25. Prepare for Post-Release Support

Plan for Post-Release Testing: Develop a plan for post-release testing to monitor the software's performance and address any issues that may arise after deployment.

Establish a Support Process: Set up a process for handling user-reported issues, including a mechanism for tracking, prioritizing, and resolving post-release defects.

By incorporating these additional points, the software testing process becomes even more comprehensive and effective, leading to higher-quality software and improved user satisfaction. These guidelines ensure that testing efforts are thorough, well-organized, and aligned with best practices, ultimately contributing to the overall success of the project.

2.5. Overview of the Software Testing Process

The software testing process is a systematic approach aimed at ensuring that software applications meet specified requirements and quality standards. It begins with requirement analysis, where the focus is on understanding and documenting the software's requirements and specifications. This stage involves reviewing functional and non-functional requirements, user stories, and business rules to ensure they are clear and testable, and establishing clear testing objectives that align with these requirements.

Following this, the test planning phase involves creating a comprehensive plan that outlines the testing strategy, scope, resources, and schedule. This includes defining the overall approach to testing, such as types of testing required, tools, and techniques, and developing a detailed test plan that includes test objectives, scope, resource allocation, and deliverables. Roles and responsibilities are assigned to ensure accountability and effective execution.

In the test design phase, detailed test cases and scenarios are developed based on the requirements and test plan. Test cases specify the inputs, execution steps, and expected outcomes for each functionality, while test scenarios outline broader user journeys and high-level functionalities. Test data is also prepared to ensure it reflects real-world usage and conditions.

The test environment setup phase focuses on preparing the testing environment to accurately replicate production conditions. This involves configuring hardware, software, network, and database settings to match the production environment and managing test data to ensure its accuracy and relevance.

During test execution, test cases and scenarios are executed to identify defects and validate software functionality. Manual testing is performed for scenarios requiring human judgment, such as exploratory or usability testing, while automated testing is used for repetitive tasks like regression or load testing. Results are recorded, including pass/fail status, deviations from expected results, and defects encountered.

Defect management is crucial for addressing and resolving identified issues. Defects are logged in a defect tracking system with detailed information, including steps to reproduce, severity, and impact. They are then prioritized and assigned to developers for resolution, and progress is monitored to ensure defects are addressed. Fixed issues are retested to confirm resolution.

Regression testing is conducted to verify that recent changes or fixes have not introduced new defects or affected existing functionality. This involves running previously executed test cases and updating them as needed to reflect software changes.

The final validation phase ensures that the software meets all requirements and is ready for release. This includes conducting User Acceptance Testing (UAT) to confirm that the software meets user expectations and obtaining formal sign-off from stakeholders to approve the software for production deployment.

Test closure involves completing the testing process and documenting outcomes for future reference. This includes reviewing testing activities to evaluate effectiveness, preparing detailed test reports, and conducting a retrospective to identify lessons learned and areas for improvement.

Post-release testing monitors the software's performance and stability in the production environment. This phase includes handling user feedback, addressing any defects or issues reported post-release, and planning for future updates based on user feedback and evolving requirements.

Finally, continuous improvement focuses on enhancing the testing process based on feedback and lessons learned. This involves analyzing testing metrics to assess the effectiveness and efficiency of the testing process and implementing improvements to refine testing strategies, tools, and techniques.

By following these structured steps, organizations can build an effective software testing process that ensures high-quality software delivery, meets user expectations, and supports overall project success.

The Seven Step Software Testing Process

The Seven-Step Software Testing Process provides a structured approach to ensuring software quality and reliability through a series of well-defined stages. It begins with Test Planning, where the overall framework for testing is established. This includes defining the objectives of testing, such as validating functionality, performance, and security. A detailed test plan is created, outlining the testing strategy, scope, resources, and schedule. This phase also involves assigning roles and responsibilities to the testing team and setting criteria for success.

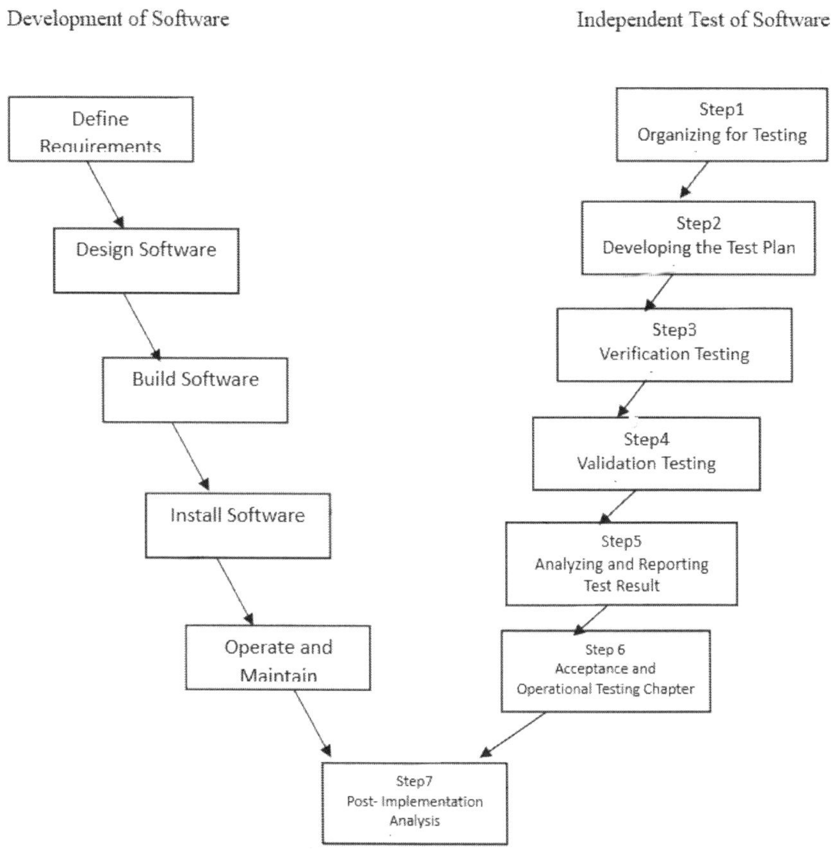

Fig 2.5.1 The seven step software testing process

Following test planning is Test Design, where detailed test cases and scenarios are developed based on the requirements outlined in the planning phase. Test cases are crafted to cover specific inputs, execution steps, and expected outcomes for each functionality or feature, ensuring comprehensive coverage of all aspects of the software. Test scenarios are created to represent broader user journeys and high-level functionalities. Additionally, realistic test data is prepared to reflect actual usage conditions, ensuring that testing is conducted under realistic scenarios.

The Test Environment Setup phase focuses on configuring the testing environment to closely replicate production conditions. This involves setting up the necessary hardware, software, network configurations, and databases. The test environment is validated to ensure that it is correctly configured and fully operational before testing begins. Preparing and managing test data is also a key component of this phase, ensuring that it is relevant and comprehensive.

During Test Execution, the prepared test cases and scenarios are executed to identify defects and validate the software's functionality. Manual testing is performed for scenarios that require human judgment, such as exploratory and usability testing. Automated tests are executed for repetitive tasks like regression and performance testing. The outcomes of test execution are documented, including pass/fail status, deviations from expected results, and details of any defects encountered.

Defect Management is a critical step that involves identifying, logging, and managing defects discovered during testing. Defects are recorded in a defect tracking system with detailed information, including steps to reproduce, severity, and impact. Defects are prioritized based on their severity and impact, and assigned to developers for resolution. The progress of defect resolution is monitored, and fixed issues are retested to confirm that defects have been addressed effectively.

After managing defects, Regression Testing is performed to ensure that recent changes or fixes have not introduced new defects or negatively impacted existing functionality. This involves re-running previously executed test cases to verify that the software remains stable and reliable after changes. Test cases are updated or modified as needed to reflect changes in the software.

The final step is Test Closure, which involves completing the testing process and documenting the outcomes. This phase includes reviewing the effectiveness of the testing activities, preparing final test reports, and conducting a retrospective to identify lessons learned and areas for improvement. Test artifacts, such as test plans, test cases, defect logs, and test reports, are archived for future reference and maintenance.

By following these seven steps—Test Planning, Test Design, Test Environment Setup, Test Execution, Defect Management, Regression Testing, and Test Closure—organizations can ensure a thorough and effective testing process. This structured approach helps deliver high-quality software that meets user expectations and maintains reliability throughout its lifecycle.

UNIT 3

TESTING PROCESS

3.1. Organizing for Testing

Ensures that all aspects of the testing environment, resources, team roles, and test planning are thoroughly prepared and structured. This phase includes setting up the workbench, allocating resources, organizing the team, and developing a detailed test plan. Proper organization enhances the efficiency, consistency, and effectiveness of the testing process, leading to more reliable and actionable results.

By focusing on these aspects, teams can create a robust foundation for successful testing and quality assurance.

3.2. Workbench Overview

The workbench is where all the testing activities are conducted. It includes the setup of hardware and software resources, configuration of testing tools, and management of test data. Properly organizing and configuring the workbench ensures that testing is carried out efficiently, effectively, and with minimal disruptions.

1. Physical Workbench Setup

Definition: The physical workbench includes the tangible infrastructure and hardware components needed to perform testing. This setup must support the physical needs of the testers and the requirements of the test cases.

Components:

- **Hardware:**
    - » **Test Machines:** These include computers, servers, and any devices where the application will be tested. Machines should be equipped with adequate specifications to handle the test workload.

  - **Network Equipment:** Routers, switches, and cables that ensure network connectivity for testing applications that require internet or intranet access.
  - **Peripheral Devices:** Printers, scanners, or other external devices that the software might interact with.
- **Workspace:**
  - **Physical Layout:** A well-organized physical space where testing will be conducted, including desks, chairs, and other ergonomic considerations.
  - **Environmental Conditions:** Ensure proper lighting, ventilation, and temperature control to create a comfortable working environment.

Best Practices:

- **Consistent Setup:** Maintain a consistent setup across different testing environments to ensure comparability of results.
- **Ergonomics:** Design the workspace to be comfortable and efficient for testers, minimizing physical strain and maximizing productivity.
- **Maintenance:** Regularly check and maintain physical equipment to avoid unexpected failures during testing.

2. Virtual Workbench Setup

Definition: The virtual workbench involves the setup of software environments and tools required for testing. This includes configuring operating systems, applications, and testing tools in a virtual or cloud-based environment.

Components:

- **Software Tools:**
  - **Testing Tools:** Automated testing tools (e.g., Selenium, TestComplete), performance testing tools (e.g., JMeter), and test management tools (e.g., TestRail).
  - **Development Tools:** Integrated Development Environments (IDEs) and version control systems (e.g., Git).
  - **Monitoring Tools:** Tools for monitoring application performance and system health (e.g., New Relic).
- **Virtual Environments:**
  - **Virtual Machines (VMs):** Use VMs to simulate different operating systems and configurations. VMs can be quickly created and modified as needed.
  - **Cloud Services:** Platforms like AWS, Azure, or Google Cloud to provide scalable and on-demand testing environments.

- **Configuration Management:**
  - » **Configuration Files:** Manage and maintain configuration files required for different test environments.
  - » **Environment Variables:** Set and manage environment variables specific to testing needs.

Best Practices:

- **Environment Parity:** Ensure virtual environments closely match production environments to get accurate test results.
- **Scalability:** Use cloud services to easily scale resources based on testing requirements.
- **Documentation:** Document the setup and configuration of virtual environments for consistency and reproducibility.

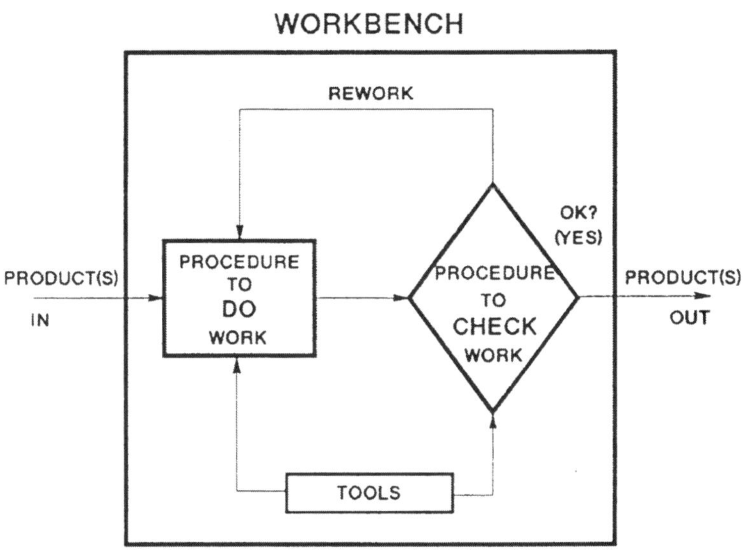

Fig 3.2.1 The workbench for testing software.

3. Test Data Management

Definition: Test data management involves creating, organizing, and maintaining the data used for testing. Proper management ensures that test data is relevant, accurate, and secure.

Components:

- Test Data Creation:
  - » **Data Generation:** Create data sets that simulate real-world scenarios and cover various test cases.

- » **Data Masking:** Mask sensitive data to ensure privacy and compliance with regulations.
- Data Storage:
  - » **Databases:** Use databases to store and manage test data. Ensure that data is easily accessible and well-organized.
  - » **Backup:** Regularly back up test data to prevent loss and ensure data integrity.
- Data Management Tools:
  - » **Data Management Systems:** Tools for managing and organizing test data (e.g., Data Factory).
  - » **Test Data Generators:** Tools for automating the creation of test data (e.g., Mockaroo).

Best Practices:

- **Data Relevance:** Ensure that test data is relevant to the scenarios being tested.
- **Data Security:** Protect test data, especially if it includes sensitive information.
- **Data Consistency:** Maintain consistency in test data across different test environments.

4. Test Tools and Utilities

Definition: Test tools and utilities are the software components used to facilitate and automate various aspects of the testing process.

Components:

- **Test Automation Tools:**
  - » **Functional Testing:** Tools for automating functional tests (e.g., Selenium, QTP).
  - » **Performance Testing:** Tools for load and performance testing (e.g., LoadRunner, JMeter).
- **Test Management Tools:**
  - » **Test Case Management:** Tools for creating and managing test cases (e.g., TestRail, Zephyr).
  - » **Defect Tracking:** Tools for tracking and managing defects (e.g., Jira, Bugzilla).
- **Utility Tools:**
  - » **Monitoring Tools:** Tools for monitoring system performance and logs (e.g., Splunk, Grafana).

- » **Data Generation Tools:** Tools for generating test data (e.g., Faker, Mockaroo).

Best Practices:

- **Tool Integration:** Ensure that tools are well-integrated to streamline testing processes.
- **Tool Selection:** Choose tools based on the specific needs of the project and the testing requirements.
- **Training:** Provide training to team members on how to effectively use the tools.

5. Test Environment Configuration

Definition: Configuring the test environment involves setting up the software, hardware, and network configurations necessary to support testing activities.

Components:

- **Software Configuration:**
  - » **Installation:** Install necessary software and tools in the test environment.
  - » **Configuration Files:** Set up and manage configuration files for different test scenarios.
- **Hardware Configuration:**
  - » **System Requirements:** Ensure that hardware meets the system requirements for running tests.
  - » **Network Configuration:** Configure network settings to support connectivity and communication between test components.
- Network Configuration:
  - » **Firewalls and Security:** Configure firewalls and security settings to ensure safe and proper communication.
  - » **Network Access:** Ensure that test environments have proper network access to external systems if needed.

Best Practices:

- **Environment Consistency:** Maintain consistency in configurations across different environments (development, staging, production).
- **Documentation:** Document configurations to facilitate setup and troubleshooting.

- **Testing Configurations:** Regularly review and update configurations based on changes in requirements or test scenarios.

The **Workbench** in the testing process encompasses the preparation and configuration of both physical and virtual environments necessary for testing. This includes:

- **Physical Setup:** Hardware, network equipment, and workspace.
- **Virtual Setup:** Software tools, virtual environments, and configuration management.
- **Test Data Management:** Creation, storage, and management of test data.
- **Test Tools and Utilities:** Automation tools, management tools, and utility tools.

1. Procedure

Definition: In the context of testing, the procedure refers to the systematic steps and methods used to perform testing activities. This includes defining how tests are executed, managed, and reported, ensuring consistency and reliability in the testing process.

Components:

Test Preparation

- **Define Objectives:**
  - » Clarify the goals of the test, including what is being validated or verified.
  - » Objectives could include functional correctness, performance benchmarks, or security compliance.
- **Prepare Test Environment:**
  - » Set up the required hardware, software, and network configurations.
  - » Ensure that the environment mirrors the production setup as closely as possible.
- **Create Test Data:**
  - » Develop or gather test data needed to execute test cases.
  - » Ensure that data is realistic and representative of real-world scenarios.

Test Execution

- **Execute Test Cases:**
  - » Run the test cases according to the test plan.
  - » Follow the steps defined in the test cases and record the outcomes.

- Monitor Testing:
  - » Monitor the test execution to ensure that tests are running as expected.
  - » Address any issues or interruptions that occur during testing.

Test Reporting

- **Log Defects:**
  - » Record any issues or defects found during testing.
  - » Include details such as steps to reproduce, severity, and screenshots if applicable.
- **Report Test Results:**
  - » Summarize the outcomes of the tests, including pass/fail status and any defects found.
  - » Prepare reports for stakeholders, highlighting key findings and any areas of concern.

Post-Test Activities

- Review and Retest:
  - » Review the defects and issues identified during testing.
  - » Retest fixed issues and verify that they have been resolved.
- Document Lessons Learned:
  - » Capture lessons learned from the testing process to improve future testing efforts.
  - » Document any issues with the testing procedure or environment.

Best Practices:

- **Consistency:** Ensure that the testing procedure is consistent across different test cycles and environments.
- **Documentation:** Maintain detailed documentation of the procedures followed during testing for transparency and reproducibility.
- **Automation:** Where possible, automate repetitive tasks to improve efficiency and accuracy.

2. Developing the Test Plan

Definition: Developing a test plan involves creating a detailed document that outlines the testing strategy, objectives, scope, resources, schedule, and procedures. A well-defined test plan serves as a roadmap for the testing process and ensures alignment with project goals and requirements.

Components:

Test Plan Overview

- **Test Objectives:**
  - » Define the goals and purpose of the testing.
  - » Objectives could include validating functionality, ensuring performance, or verifying security.
- Scope:
  - » Detail what will be included and excluded from the testing process.
  - » Define the boundaries of the testing effort.

Test Strategy

- **Test Types:**
  - » Specify the types of testing to be conducted, such as unit testing, integration testing, system testing, and acceptance testing.
- **Testing Levels:**
  - » Define the levels of testing, including unit tests, integration tests, system tests, and end-to-end tests.

Test Scope and Boundaries

- **In-Scope:**
  - » Detail the features, functionalities, and systems that will be tested.
  - » Identify specific requirements or components that will be included in the testing.
- **Out-of-Scope:**
  - » Specify what will not be tested to avoid misunderstandings and scope creep.

Resource Allocation

- **Personnel:**
  - » Identify the team members involved in testing and their roles.
  - » Define responsibilities and allocate tasks based on expertise.
- **Tools and Technologies:**
  - » List the tools and technologies required for testing, such as automation tools, test management tools, and performance testing tools.

Schedule and Milestones

- Timeline:
  - » Create a timeline for the testing activities, including start and end dates.
  - » Define key milestones and deadlines for different phases of the testing process.
- **Test Execution Schedule:**
  - » Plan the schedule for executing test cases and conducting different types of testing.

Risk Management

- **Identify Risks:**
  - » Identify potential risks that could impact the testing process, such as resource constraints or technical challenges.
- **Mitigation Strategies:**
  - » Develop strategies to mitigate identified risks and address potential issues proactively.

Test Deliverables

- **Deliverables:**
  - » Define the deliverables expected from the testing process, such as test cases, test results, defect reports, and final test reports.
- **Acceptance Criteria:**
  - » Specify the criteria for test acceptance and how the success of testing will be measured.

Best Practices:

- **Clarity:** Ensure that the test plan is clear and detailed, covering all aspects of the testing process.
- **Stakeholder Review:** Have the test plan reviewed and approved by stakeholders to ensure alignment with project goals.
- **Flexibility:** Allow for adjustments in the test plan as project requirements or conditions change.

Procedure: This involves the systematic steps required to prepare for, execute, and report on testing activities. It includes test preparation, execution, reporting, and post-test activities, ensuring a structured and consistent approach to testing.

Developing the Test Plan: This involves creating a comprehensive document that outlines the testing strategy, scope, resources, schedule, and procedures. A well-developed test plan serves as a roadmap for the testing process, ensuring that all aspects of testing are covered and aligned with project goals.

Both components are integral to ensuring that testing is conducted effectively, providing reliable results and contributing to the overall quality of the software.

3.3. Verification Testing

Definition: Verification testing is a type of testing that confirms whether the product or system meets the defined specifications and design requirements. It is a process of evaluating whether the software or system complies with the requirements and design specifications established before development.

Purpose: The main goal of verification testing is to ensure that the product or system is built correctly according to the requirements and design documents. It helps identify defects early in the development cycle and ensures that the product behaves as expected.

1. Verification Testing Types

Verification testing can be performed through various types of tests, including:

Static Testing

Definition: Static testing involves examining the product without executing it. This includes reviewing documents, code, and design artifacts to ensure they meet the specified requirements.

Components:

- **Code Reviews:**
  - » **Description:** Manual inspection of code by developers or peers to identify issues or deviations from coding standards.
  - » **Purpose:** To catch defects early and ensure adherence to coding practices.
- **Static Analysis:**
  - » **Description:** Automated tools analyze the codebase for potential issues such as security vulnerabilities, code complexity, or style violations.
  - » **Purpose:** To identify problems that may not be easily visible through manual inspection.
- **Documentation Reviews:**
  - » **Description:** Examination of requirement documents, design specifications, and other relevant documents.

» **Purpose:** To ensure that all requirements are correctly captured and that the documentation is complete and accurate.

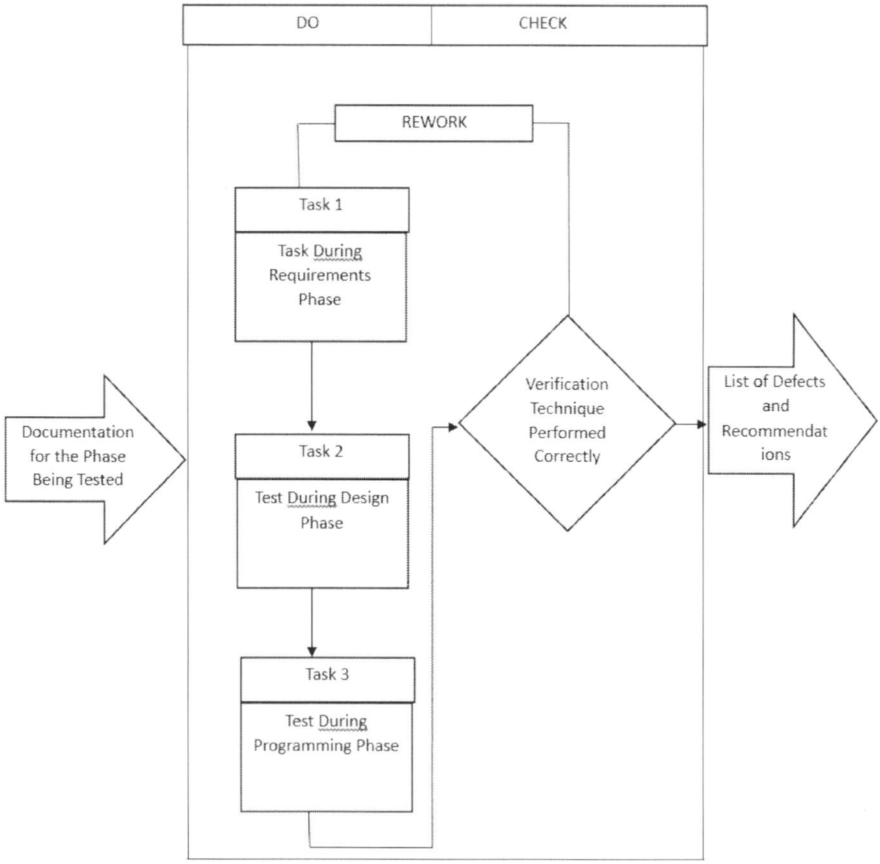

Fig 3.1.1 Workbench for verification testing.

Dynamic Testing

Definition: Dynamic testing involves executing the software or system to verify that it functions according to the specified requirements.

Components:

- **Unit Testing:**
  » **Description:** Testing individual components or functions of the software to ensure they work as intended.

  » **Purpose:** To verify that each unit performs correctly in isolation.

- **Integration Testing:**
  - » **Description:** Testing interactions between integrated components or systems to ensure they work together properly.
  - » **Purpose:** To identify issues related to interfaces and data flow between components.
- **System Testing:**
  - » **Description:** Testing the entire system as a whole to ensure it meets the specified requirements and performs as expected.
  - » **Purpose:** To validate the end-to-end functionality of the system.
- **Acceptance Testing:**
  - » **Description:** Testing to determine if the system meets the business requirements and is ready for deployment.
  - » **Purpose:** To ensure that the system meets the needs of the end-users and stakeholders.

2. Verification Testing Process

Requirement Analysis

Definition: The process starts with analyzing the requirements and design specifications to ensure that they are complete, clear, and testable.

Components:

- **Requirement Gathering:**
  - » **Description:** Collecting all relevant requirements from stakeholders and documentation.
  - » **Purpose:** To have a clear understanding of what needs to be verified.
- **Requirement Review:**
  - » **Description:** Reviewing requirements to ensure they are feasible, complete, and unambiguous.
  - » **Purpose:** To identify any gaps or inconsistencies in the requirements.

Test Planning

Definition: Creating a detailed plan that outlines the scope, objectives, resources, and schedule for verification testing.

Components:

- **Test Plan Creation:**
  - » **Description:** Developing a test plan that includes test objectives, scope, resources, and schedule.
  - » **Purpose:** To provide a roadmap for the verification testing process.

- **Test Case Development:**
  - » **Description:** Creating test cases based on requirements and design documents.
  - » **Purpose:** To define the conditions and steps for verifying each requirement.

Test Execution

Definition: Executing the test cases and verifying that the software or system meets the specified requirements.

Components:

- **Execute Test Cases:**
  - » **Description:** Running the test cases to validate that the product meets the design specifications.
  - » **Purpose:** To confirm that each requirement is correctly implemented.
- **Record Results:**
  - » **Description:** Documenting the outcomes of the tests, including pass/fail status and any issues encountered.
  - » **Purpose:** To provide evidence of the verification process and identify any defects.

Defect Management

Definition: Managing and addressing any defects or issues identified during verification testing.

Components:

- **Log Defects:**
  - » **Description:** Recording defects found during testing, including details and steps to reproduce.
  - » **Purpose:** To track issues and facilitate resolution.
- **Defect Resolution:**
  - » **Description:** Working with the development team to fix defects and retest as necessary.
  - » **Purpose:** To ensure that all identified issues are addressed and resolved.

Test Reporting

Definition: Preparing reports that summarize the results of verification testing and provide insights into the quality of the product.

Components:

- **Test Summary Report:**
    - » **Description:** Summarizing the outcomes of the verification testing, including pass/fail rates and defect status.
    - » **Purpose:** To provide stakeholders with an overview of the testing results.
- **Detailed Defect Report:**
    - » **Description:** Detailed documentation of defects found, including severity, impact, and resolution status.
    - » **Purpose:** To offer a detailed view of issues encountered and their status.

3. Best Practices for Verification Testing

- **Early Verification:** Start verification testing early in the development cycle to catch issues as soon as possible.
- **Comprehensive Coverage:** Ensure that all requirements and design specifications are covered by test cases.
- **Automation:** Where feasible, use automated testing tools to improve efficiency and consistency in verification testing.
- **Documentation:** Maintain thorough documentation of test cases, execution results, and defects to provide transparency and traceability.
- **Continuous Improvement:** Regularly review and improve the verification process based on feedback and lessons learned.

Summary

Verification Testing is a critical part of the software development lifecycle aimed at ensuring that the product or system is built according to its requirements and design specifications. It involves various types of testing such as static and dynamic testing, and follows a structured process including requirement analysis, test planning, execution, defect management, and reporting. Effective verification testing helps in identifying and resolving issues early, ensuring that the product meets its intended requirements and functions correctly.

Workbench for Testing

The workbench refers to the tools, environments, and infrastructure used during the testing process. It is critical for both verification and validation testing to ensure that the tests are accurate, repeatable, and relevant to the product's intended use.

Components of the Workbench:

1. Hardware:

- **Test Machines:** Computers, servers, or devices where the software or product is deployed for testing.
- **Network Equipment:** Routers, switches, and other networking devices needed to simulate different network conditions.
- **Peripheral Devices:** Any additional hardware required for testing, such as printers, scanners, or specialized equipment relevant to the product.

2. Software:

- **Test Management Tools:** Software used to plan, execute, and track testing activities (e.g., JIRA, TestRail).
- **Automated Testing Tools:** Tools that facilitate automated testing, such as Selenium, QTP, or Jenkins.
- **Debugging Tools:** Software used to identify, analyze, and resolve issues within the product (e.g., GDB, WinDbg).
- **Virtualization Software:** Tools that allow the creation of virtual environments for testing (e.g., VMware, VirtualBox).

3. Environment:

- **Development Environment:** Where the product is initially developed and unit tested.
- **Testing/Staging Environment:** A controlled environment that closely mirrors the production environment for executing verification and validation tests.
- **Production Environment:** The live environment where the product will ultimately be deployed.

4. Data:

- **Test Data:** Data specifically created for testing purposes to validate different scenarios.
- **Mock Data:** Simulated data used to mimic real-world data without the need for actual user data.
- **Data Management Tools:** Tools used to create, manage, and reset test data (e.g., data generators, database management systems).

5. Procedures and Protocols:

- **Standard Operating Procedures (SOPs):** Documented processes for conducting tests, reporting issues, and managing changes.

- **Version Control:** Systems to manage and track changes in the code and documentation (e.g., Git, SVN).
- **Continuous Integration/Continuous Deployment (CI/CD):** Practices and tools that automate the integration and deployment of code changes, ensuring continuous testing and delivery.

Setting Up the Workbench:

1. Define Requirements:

- Understand the hardware, software, and environment requirements for the product.
- Document the specifications needed for the testing infrastructure.

2. Procure and Configure Hardware:

- Set up test machines and network equipment according to the documented requirements.
- Ensure all peripheral devices are available and properly configured.

3. Install and Configure Software:

- Deploy test management and automated testing tools.
- Set up debugging and virtualization software.
- Ensure all software is correctly configured and integrated.

4. Create and Manage Environments:

- Set up development, testing, staging, and production environments.
- Use virtualization to create isolated and repeatable test environments.
- Ensure environments closely mirror real-world conditions for accurate validation.

5. Prepare Test Data:

- Create test and mock data that covers all possible scenarios.
- Use data management tools to handle test data efficiently.

6. Establish Procedures:

- Document all testing procedures and protocols.
- Implement version control and CI/CD practices to manage code changes and testing cycles.

7. Monitor and Maintain:

- Regularly monitor the workbench to ensure it meets testing needs.
- Maintain hardware and software, updating and upgrading as necessary.

- Continuously improve procedures based on feedback and evolving requirements.

By ensuring that the workbench is well-equipped and properly configured, you can create a robust testing environment that supports both verification and validation processes effectively.

1. Verification Testing Procedure

Verification testing focuses on ensuring that each stage of development meets the specified requirements. It is generally conducted in a controlled environment to check the internal consistency and quality of the product.

Step-by-Step Procedure:

1. Requirements Review:

- **Objective:** Ensure that all requirements are documented, clear, and traceable.
- **Activities:**
  - » Gather all requirement documents.
  - » Create a traceability matrix linking requirements to specific test cases.
  - » Review requirements with stakeholders to clarify any ambiguities.

2. Test Case Development:

- **Objective:** Develop detailed test cases that cover all requirements.
- **Activities:**
  - » Identify test scenarios based on requirements.
  - » Write detailed test cases, including inputs, execution steps, and expected results.
  - » Review and validate test cases with the development and QA teams.

3. Test Environment Setup:

- Objective: Prepare the testing environment to ensure it mirrors the development environment.
- Activities:
  - » Configure hardware and software as per requirements.
  - » Install necessary tools and applications.
  - » Ensure the environment is stable and ready for testing.

4. Test Execution:

- **Objective:** Execute the test cases and record results.

- **Activities:**
  - » Run each test case according to the defined steps.
  - » Document the actual outcomes and compare them to the expected results.
  - » Capture screenshots, logs, or any other evidence of test execution.

5. Defect Reporting and Management:

- **Objective:** Identify and report any discrepancies or defects.
- **Activities:**
  - » Log defects in a defect tracking tool.
  - » Provide detailed information including steps to reproduce, severity, and impact.
  - » Collaborate with the development team for defect resolution.

6. Regression Testing:

- **Objective:** Ensure that new code changes do not adversely affect existing functionalities.
- **Activities:**
  - » Re-run previously passed test cases that could be affected by the new changes.
  - » Verify that defects are fixed and no new issues are introduced.
  - » Document results and update test cases if necessary.

Validation Testing Procedure

Validation testing ensures that the final product meets user needs and requirements. It is conducted in a real-world or simulated environment to validate the product's performance, usability, and satisfaction.

Step-by-Step Procedure:

1. User Requirements Review:

- **Objective:** Confirm all user requirements are clearly understood and documented.
- **Activities:**
  - » Review user stories, use cases, and requirement documents.
  - » Ensure all requirements are linked to specific test scenarios.
  - » Validate requirements with end-users and stakeholders.

2. Test Case Development:

- **Objective:** Create test cases that simulate real-world user scenarios.
- **Activities:**
  - » Develop detailed test cases based on user requirements.
  - » Include usability and performance criteria.
  - » Review and validate test cases with stakeholders and end-users.

3. Test Environment Setup:

- **Objective:** Prepare an environment that simulates the production environment.
- **Activities:**
  - » Configure hardware and software to reflect the actual user environment.
  - » Install and configure any additional tools or applications required.
  - » Ensure data is populated to reflect real-world scenarios.

4. Test Execution:

- **Objective:** Execute the test cases and gather feedback from users.
- **Activities:**
  - » Conduct tests in the real-world or simulated environment.
  - » Observe user interactions and gather feedback.
  - » Document actual outcomes and compare them to expected results.

5. User Acceptance Testing (UAT):

- Objective: Validate the product with actual users.
- Activities:
  - » Plan and schedule UAT sessions with selected users.
  - » Provide users with scenarios and tasks to perform.
  - » Collect user feedback on performance, usability, and satisfaction.

6. Defect Reporting and Resolution:

- **Objective:** Identify and resolve any issues found during validation.
- **Activities:**
  - » Log defects and issues reported by users.
  - » Prioritize and assign defects for resolution.
  - » Retest resolved defects to ensure they are fixed.

7. Final Validation:

- **Objective:** Ensure all user requirements are met and obtain formal approval.
- **Activities:**
  - » Review all test results and user feedback.
  - » Ensure all critical defects are resolved.
  - » Obtain sign-off from stakeholders and end-users for product release.

Workbench in Software Testing

The term "workbench" in the context of software testing refers to the setup and environment used to facilitate the testing process. This includes the hardware, software, tools, and documentation necessary to conduct thorough and effective testing.

Components of a Workbench

Hardware Components:

1. Servers and Desktops:

- **Purpose:** Used to create and manage test environments where tests are executed.
- **Example:** A server might host a test management tool, while desktops are used by testers to run test cases.

2. Mobile Devices:

- **Purpose:** Necessary for testing applications on different platforms (iOS, Android) and configurations.
- **Example:** Multiple devices with varying OS versions to ensure compatibility and performance.

3. Network Equipment:

- **Purpose:** Simulates different network conditions such as varying bandwidth, latency, and packet loss.
- **Example:** Routers and switches that help replicate different network environments.

4. Peripheral Devices:

- **Purpose:** Ensures compatibility with external devices the software must interact with.
- **Example:** Printers, scanners, and specialized equipment like biometric scanners.

Software Components:

1. Test Management Tools:

- **Purpose:** Plan, execute, and track testing activities.
- **Example:** JIRA, TestRail, HP ALM.

2. Automation Tools:

- **Purpose:** Automate repetitive test cases to save time and reduce errors.
- **Example:** Selenium, Appium, QTP.

3. Debugging Tools:

- Purpose: Identify, analyze, and resolve issues in the software.
- Example:GDB, WinDbg, Chrome DevTools.

4. Continuous Integration Tools:

- **Purpose:** Automate the integration and testing of code changes.
- **Example:** Jenkins, Travis CI, Bamboo.

5. Static Analysis Tools:

- **Purpose:** Analyze code quality and detect potential issues.
- **Example:** SonarQube, Coverity.

6. Virtualization Software:

- **Purpose:** Create virtual environments for testing.
- **Example:** VMware, VirtualBox, Docker.

Documentation Tools:

1. Requirement Management Tools:

- **Purpose:** Manage and trace requirements throughout the testing lifecycle.
- **Example:** IBM DOORS, Jama Software.

2. Version Control Systems:

- **Purpose:** Manage and track changes in code and documentation.
- **Example:** Git, SVN, Mercurial.

3. Communication Tools:

- **Purpose:** Facilitate effective communication and collaboration among team members.
- **Example:** Slack, Microsoft Teams, Zoom.

4. Documentation Tools:

- **Purpose:** Create and maintain test plan documents, reports, and other relevant documentation.
- **Example:** MS Word, Google Docs, MS Excel, Google Sheets.

Setting Up the Workbench

1. Define Objectives and Scope:

- Clearly outline what the testing process aims to achieve and the extent of the testing activities.

2. Select Appropriate Tools and Hardware:

- Choose tools and hardware that best meet the testing requirements. Ensure compatibility and scalability to handle different test scenarios.

3. Configure Test Environments:

- Set up environments that closely mirror the production environment to ensure realistic testing conditions.

4. Establish Documentation Standards:

- Develop templates and guidelines for creating and maintaining test plans, test cases, and other documentation.

5. Implement Automation:

- Use automation tools to streamline repetitive tasks and focus manual testing efforts on complex scenarios.

6. Integrate with CI/CD Pipelines:

- Ensure that the workbench is integrated with continuous integration/continuous deployment pipelines to automate the testing of code changes.

7. Regular Maintenance and Updates:

- Keep the workbench updated with the latest tools, hardware, and configurations to ensure effective testing.

Benefits of a Well-Configured Workbench

1. Efficiency: Streamlines the testing process, reducing time and effort required for test execution and management.

2. Accuracy: Ensures accurate and reliable test results by providing realistic test environments and scenarios.

3. Scalability: Allows for easy scaling of testing activities to handle larger projects and more complex test cases.

4. Collaboration: Facilitates effective communication and collaboration among team members, leading to better coordination and faster issue resolution.

5. Traceability: Provides clear traceability of requirements, test cases, and defects, ensuring comprehensive coverage and accountability.

Procedure for Software Testing

The procedure for software testing encompasses a series of systematic steps designed to ensure that software products meet specified requirements and function correctly. This procedure serves as a framework to guide testing activities and maintain quality throughout the software development lifecycle.

1. Define the Testing Objectives

Purpose:

- Clearly outline the goals and objectives of the testing process.

Steps:

- Identify what needs to be validated (functional requirements, performance criteria, user acceptance).
- Determine the success criteria for the testing process.
- Engage stakeholders to ensure alignment on testing goals.

2. Develop a Testing Strategy

Purpose:

- Create a high-level plan that outlines the approach for testing.
- Steps:
- Determine the types of testing to be performed (unit, integration, system, acceptance).
- Define the testing levels and phases.
- Select appropriate testing methodologies (manual, automated, exploratory).
- Identify tools and resources required for testing.

3. Create a Test Plan

Purpose:

- Document the detailed plan for testing, including scope, schedule, resources, and deliverables.

Steps:

- **Define Scope:** Specify the features and functionalities to be tested.

- **Identify Deliverables:** List all testing deliverables (test cases, test data, defect reports).
- **Develop Schedule:** Create a timeline for testing activities, including milestones and deadlines.
- **Allocate Resources:** Assign roles and responsibilities to team members.
- **Identify Risks:** Assess potential risks that could impact testing and develop mitigation strategies.

4. Set Up Test Environments

Purpose:

- Create a controlled environment where testing can be conducted.

Steps:

- Configure hardware and software to mirror the production environment as closely as possible.
- Ensure the availability of necessary tools and resources in the testing environment.
- Populate the environment with relevant test data.
- Conduct checks to ensure the environment is stable and ready for testing.

5. Design and Develop Test Cases

Purpose:

- Create detailed test cases that specify how to validate the software.
- Steps:
- Analyze requirements and develop test cases that cover all functional and non-functional aspects.
- Include details in each test case, such as inputs, execution steps, expected outcomes, and acceptance criteria.
- Review test cases with stakeholders to ensure they are comprehensive and aligned with project requirements.

6. Execute Test Cases

Purpose:

- Perform the actual testing of the software based on the developed test cases.

Steps:

- Execute test cases in the defined test environments.

- Document actual outcomes and compare them to expected results.
- Log any defects or issues encountered during testing in a defect tracking tool, providing detailed information.

7. Conduct Regression Testing

Purpose:

- Ensure that recent changes or bug fixes have not adversely affected existing functionalities.

Steps:

- Re-execute previously passed test cases after code changes.
- Focus on areas impacted by the changes, as well as critical functionalities.
- Document and report any new defects found during regression testing.

8. Perform User Acceptance Testing (UAT)

Purpose:

- Validate the software from the end-user's perspective to ensure it meets their needs.

Steps:

- Plan and schedule UAT sessions with selected users.
- Provide users with tasks and scenarios to execute.
- Gather feedback on the product's usability, performance, and overall satisfaction.
- Document any issues or suggestions for improvement.

9. Log and Manage Defects

Purpose:

- Track defects identified during testing for resolution.

Steps:

- Log defects in a defect tracking tool, categorizing them based on severity and priority.
- Collaborate with the development team to ensure defects are resolved.
- Retest fixed defects to confirm resolution and ensure no new issues have been introduced.

10. Monitor and Report Testing Progress

Purpose:

- Provide visibility into the testing process and ensure it stays on track.

Steps:

- Use test management tools to track test case execution status and defect metrics.
- Generate regular status reports for stakeholders, highlighting progress, challenges, and next steps.
- Conduct review meetings to discuss testing results and address any issues.

11. Final Review and Validation

Purpose:

- Ensure that all testing activities are complete and the product is ready for release.

Steps:

- Conduct a final review of test results, defect status, and user feedback.
- Ensure that all critical issues are resolved and acceptance criteria are met.
- Obtain sign-off from stakeholders confirming that the product is ready for deployment.

12. Post-Release Testing and Maintenance

Purpose:

- Monitor the product in the production environment and address any issues that arise.

Steps:

- Conduct post-release testing to validate the product's performance in real-world conditions.
- Gather user feedback and address any defects or enhancement requests.
- Continuously improve testing processes and methodologies based on lessons learned.

3.4. Validation Testing: Workbench and Procedure

Validation testing is a crucial phase in the software testing process aimed at ensuring that the software product meets the user's needs and requirements. It verifies that the system operates in real-world scenarios as intended, providing confidence that the software is ready for deployment. This section elaborates on the workbench setup for validation testing and the detailed procedure to carry it out effectively.

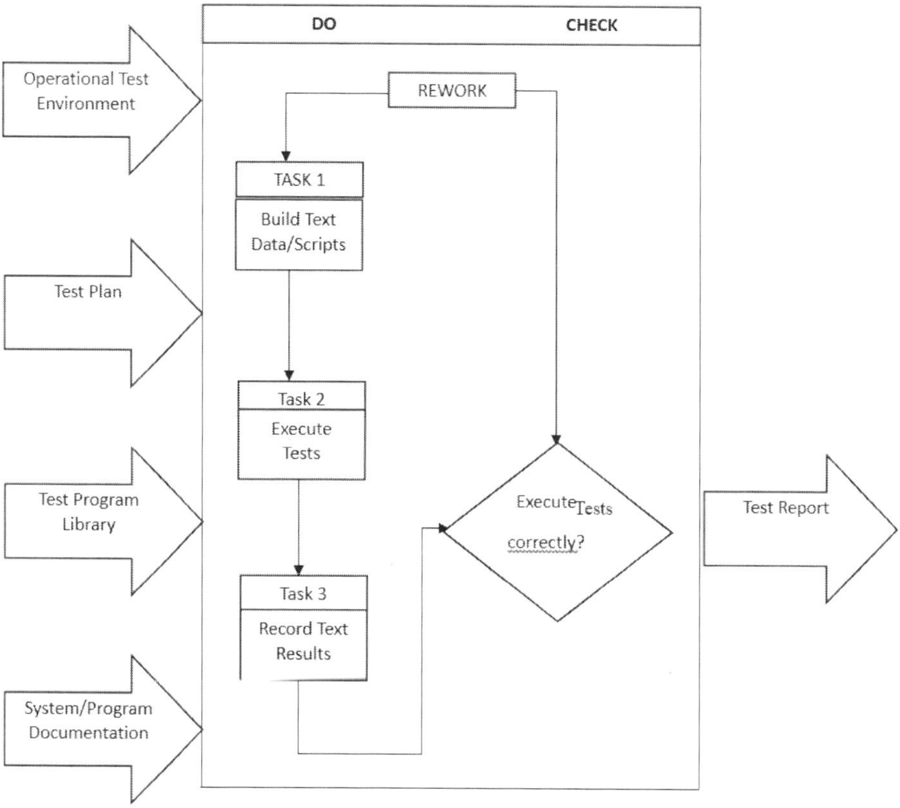

Fig 3.4.1 Workbench for Validation Testing

1. Workbench for Validation Testing

The workbench for validation testing encompasses the tools, hardware, software, and procedures necessary to perform thorough and accurate validation tests. It creates an environment where testers can simulate real-world conditions and assess the software's performance, usability, and overall functionality.

Hardware Components

1. Computers and Servers:

- Used to host the application under test and the necessary testing tools.
- Should be configured to mirror the production environment to simulate real user experiences.

2. Mobile Devices:

- Essential for testing applications designed for mobile platforms (iOS, Android).
- Different devices and OS versions should be included to ensure compatibility.

3. Network Equipment:

- Routers and switches to simulate various network conditions (bandwidth, latency, etc.).
- Helps in assessing the application's performance under different network scenarios.

4. Peripherals:

- Devices such as printers, scanners, or any other hardware the software interacts with.
- Ensures that the application integrates seamlessly with external devices.

Software Components

1. Test Management Tools:

- Tools such as JIRA, TestRail, or HP ALM for planning, executing, and tracking testing activities.
- Facilitates the organization of test cases, defect logging, and reporting.

2. Automation Testing Tools:

- Tools like Selenium, Appium, or QTP for automating repetitive test cases.
- Increases efficiency and reduces the risk of human error.

3. Performance Testing Tools:

- Tools such as JMeter or LoadRunner to assess the application's performance under load.
- Helps identify bottlenecks and performance issues.

4. Debugging and Monitoring Tools:

- Tools like GDB, WinDbg, or application performance monitoring tools to analyze issues.
- Essential for troubleshooting and ensuring the application operates as expected.

Documentation Tools

1. Requirement Management Tools:

- Tools such as IBM DOORS or Jama Software to manage and trace requirements.

- Ensures that all requirements are covered by test cases.

2. Version Control Systems:

- Git, SVN, or Mercurial to manage changes in code and documentation.
- Essential for tracking revisions and collaborating on code changes.

3. Communication Tools:

- Slack, Microsoft Teams, or Zoom for effective collaboration among team members.
- Helps in discussing test results, issues, and coordinating testing efforts.

4. Reporting Tools:

- Tools such as Excel or BI tools for generating test reports and dashboards.
- Provides stakeholders with insights into testing progress and results.

2. Procedure for Validation Testing

The procedure for validation testing consists of a series of systematic steps that guide the testing process. Each step is designed to ensure that the software meets user requirements and performs well in real-world conditions.

2.1 Step 1: Requirements Review

Purpose:

- Ensure all user requirements are clear, complete, and understood by the testing team.

Activities:

- Gather all relevant requirements, including functional and non-functional requirements.
- Create a traceability matrix to link requirements to test cases.
- Validate the requirements with stakeholders to confirm accuracy and completeness.

Step 2: Test Case Design

Purpose:

- Develop detailed test cases that will be executed during validation testing.

Activities:

- Analyze the requirements to create test cases that cover all scenarios.
- Write detailed test cases, including inputs, execution steps, expected results, and acceptance criteria.

- Review test cases with stakeholders to ensure they align with user expectations.

Step 3: Test Environment Setup

Purpose:

- Configure a controlled environment that replicates the production environment for testing.

Activities:

- Set up necessary hardware and software, including servers, databases, and network configurations.
- Install the application and any required dependencies in the test environment.
- Populate the environment with realistic test data that reflects actual usage scenarios.

Step 4: Test Execution

Purpose:

- Execute the designed test cases to validate the application.

Activities:

- Run test cases according to the defined execution plan.
- Document actual outcomes and compare them with expected results.
- Log any defects or issues found during testing in a defect tracking tool, providing detailed descriptions.

Step 5: User Acceptance Testing (UAT)

Purpose:

- Validate the software from the end-user perspective to ensure it meets their needs.

Activities:

- Schedule UAT sessions with selected users who represent the target audience.
- Provide users with tasks and scenarios to execute, gathering feedback on usability and functionality.
- Document user feedback and any issues encountered during UAT for analysis.

Step 6: Defect Logging and Management

Purpose:

- Track and manage defects identified during validation testing.

Activities:

- Log defects in a defect tracking tool, categorizing them based on severity and priority.
- Collaborate with the development team to prioritize and address defects.
- Retest fixed defects to ensure they are resolved and that no new issues were introduced.

Step 7: Final Validation

Purpose:

- Confirm that all testing activities are complete and the product is ready for release.

Activities:

- Review test results, defect status, and user feedback to ensure that all critical issues have been resolved.
- Validate that all acceptance criteria have been met.
- Obtain formal sign-off from stakeholders to confirm readiness for deployment.

Step 8: Reporting and Documentation

Purpose:

- Document the testing process, results, and any issues encountered.

Activities:

- Create comprehensive test reports summarizing test activities, outcomes, and defect statistics.
- Document lessons learned and best practices for future testing efforts.
- Share reports with stakeholders to provide visibility into the testing process and outcomes.

Step 9: Post-Release Testing and Support

Purpose:

- Monitor the product in the production environment to identify any issues that arise after release.

Activities:

- Conduct post-release testing to ensure the software functions correctly in real-world conditions.
- Gather user feedback and address any defects or enhancement requests.
- Continuously improve testing processes and methodologies based on lessons learned.

Conclusion

Validation testing is a critical component of the software development lifecycle, ensuring that products meet user requirements and perform effectively in real-world scenarios. By establishing a well-defined workbench and following a structured procedure, teams can conduct thorough validation testing that leads to high-quality software and increased user satisfaction. Effective validation testing not only identifies defects but also provides valuable insights into user experience and performance, ultimately contributing to the overall success of the software product.

UNIT 4

TESTING PROCESS

4.1 Analyzing and Reporting Test Results

Analyzing and reporting test results in software testing involves systematically examining the outcomes of executed test cases to assess the quality and reliability of the software. This process begins with a thorough review of the test data, where each test case is evaluated to determine whether it passed or failed based on the expected results. Analyzing these results helps identify defects, performance issues, or deviations from the expected behavior. Trends and patterns in failures, such as recurring bugs or problematic modules, are noted to pinpoint areas that require further investigation or improvement.

Once the analysis is complete, the findings are documented in a test report, which serves as a comprehensive record of the testing process and outcomes. This report typically includes an overview of the testing scope, objectives, and the environment in which tests were conducted. Detailed information about the test cases, including their status (pass/fail), associated defect reports, and any deviations from the planned testing activities, is also included. Metrics such as the number of tests executed, the percentage of tests passed, and the severity of identified defects provide stakeholders with a clear understanding of the software's current state.

The test report is essential for decision-making, offering insights into whether the software is ready for release, requires further development, or needs additional testing. By clearly communicating the results and their implications, the report helps ensure that stakeholders are informed about the software's quality, allowing them to make data-driven decisions that align with project goals and timelines.

4.2 Workbench

A workbench in software testing acts as a centralized hub that encapsulates the entire testing lifecycle, from planning and design to execution and reporting.

It is meticulously designed to support the diverse activities involved in testing by offering a seamless integration of tools, methodologies, and workflows that cater to both manual and automated testing needs. The workbench typically includes a test management system, where test cases are created, organized, and maintained. This system is crucial for ensuring that test cases are reusable, traceable, and aligned with the requirements of the software.

One of the core components of a testing workbench is its environment management capability. This allows testers to configure and control various test environments that mimic production settings, ensuring that tests are conducted under realistic conditions. These environments can be set up to include different operating systems, browsers, databases, and network configurations, providing comprehensive coverage and revealing potential issues that may not be evident in a single, uniform environment.

Automation is another significant aspect of a workbench, where automated test scripts are developed, executed, and maintained. The workbench often integrates with continuous integration/continuous deployment (CI/CD) pipelines, enabling automated tests to be triggered with every code change. This integration ensures that testing is continuous, helping to catch defects early in the development cycle and reducing the time and cost of fixing issues. Additionally, the workbench supports the scheduling of test runs, allowing teams to execute tests during off-peak hours or in parallel across multiple environments, further optimizing resource utilization

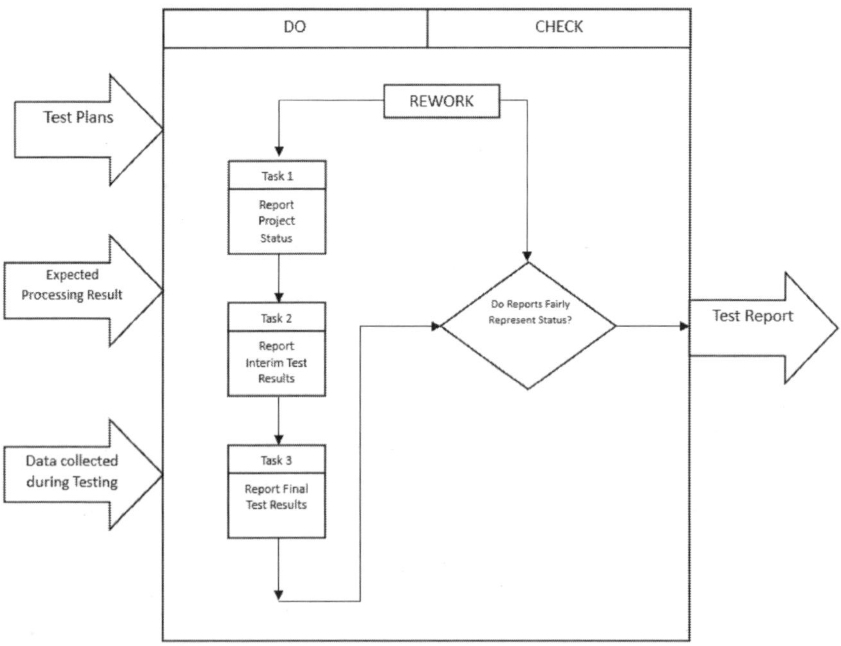

Fig 4.2.1 Analyzing and reporting test results

The workbench also includes robust defect tracking and reporting tools that are essential for maintaining quality control. These tools allow testers to log defects with detailed descriptions, steps to reproduce, and severity levels. They can be linked directly to specific test cases, providing clear traceability from requirement to defect resolution. This traceability is invaluable in regression testing, where the impact of changes or bug fixes on existing functionality needs to be assessed.

Collaboration features within a workbench are designed to facilitate communication and coordination among team members. These features may include shared dashboards, instant messaging, and version control for test artifacts, ensuring that everyone on the team is up to date with the latest test status and findings. Integration with project management tools further enhances this collaboration, allowing for better alignment between testing activities and overall project timelines.

Reporting capabilities in a workbench are comprehensive, offering real-time insights into testing progress, defect density, test coverage, and other key metrics. Customized reports can be generated for different stakeholders, providing them with the information they need to make informed decisions. These reports often include visualizations, such as graphs and charts, which make it easier to understand complex data and trends.

Finally, a well-rounded workbench is scalable and adaptable, capable of evolving with the needs of the project. It supports the addition of new tools, the customization of workflows, and the extension of its capabilities through plugins or APIs. This flexibility ensures that the workbench remains a valuable asset throughout the entire software development lifecycle, capable of supporting the testing needs of any project, regardless of its size or complexity.

4.3 Testing Software System Security

Testing software system security is an essential component of the software development lifecycle, dedicated to ensuring that the application or system is resilient against both external and internal threats. The primary goal is to uncover potential security flaws before they can be exploited, thus protecting the software from unauthorized access, data breaches, and other malicious activities. This involves a multi-faceted approach that combines various testing techniques and methodologies, each addressing different layers of the system's architecture, from the user interface to the underlying infrastructure.

One key aspect of security testing is threat modeling, a process where potential security threats are identified based on the system's design and architecture. By understanding how an attacker might approach the system, testers can focus their efforts on areas most likely to be targeted. This proactive approach helps in prioritizing testing efforts, ensuring that the most critical parts of the system are thoroughly examined.

Vulnerability assessment is another crucial step, involving the use of automated tools to scan the system for known vulnerabilities. These tools can quickly identify issues such as unpatched software, insecure configurations, or weak cryptographic practices. However, automated scans are often supplemented with manual reviews, where security experts examine the system's code and configurations for more subtle issues that automated tools might miss, such as logical flaws or misuse of cryptographic functions.

Penetration testing is a more aggressive form of security testing where testers, often referred to as ethical hackers, attempt to breach the system's defenses by exploiting the vulnerabilities found during earlier assessments. This simulated attack scenario provides valuable insights into how a real attacker could infiltrate the system and what the consequences might be. Penetration testing is typically conducted in both black-box (no prior knowledge of the system) and white-box (full knowledge of the system) modes, offering a comprehensive view of the system's security posture.

A thorough security audit is often conducted to ensure that the software complies with relevant security standards, regulations, and best practices. This includes reviewing the implementation of security controls such as authentication, authorization, encryption, and data protection mechanisms. Security auditors examine how well the system enforces access controls, manages user identities, and protects sensitive data from unauthorized access.

In addition to these proactive measures, dynamic application security testing (DAST) and static application security testing (SAST) are commonly used to assess security throughout the development process. DAST involves testing the running application in real-time, focusing on vulnerabilities that could be exploited during normal operation, such as SQL injection or cross-site scripting (XSS). On the other hand, SAST analyzes the source code, bytecode, or binary code of the software to identify vulnerabilities before the application is run. These techniques allow for the early detection and remediation of security issues, reducing the risk of vulnerabilities making it into the production environment.

Security regression testing is also important, especially after patches or updates are applied to the system. This ensures that new changes have not introduced new vulnerabilities or compromised existing security controls. Regression testing is particularly critical in agile and DevOps environments, where rapid iteration cycles can sometimes lead to security being overlooked in favor of speed.

Beyond identifying vulnerabilities, security testing also evaluates the system's incident response capabilities. This includes testing how effectively the system can detect, respond to, and recover from security incidents. Simulating attacks and breaches helps assess the robustness of the system's monitoring and logging infrastructure, the effectiveness of its incident response plans, and its ability to restore normal operations after an attack.

The culmination of all these testing activities is a comprehensive security report that provides a detailed analysis of the system's vulnerabilities, their potential impact, and prioritized recommendations for mitigation. This report is crucial for decision-makers, enabling them to understand the risks, allocate resources for remediation, and make informed decisions about the system's readiness for deployment.

Security testing is not a one-time activity but an ongoing process that continues throughout the software's lifecycle. As the threat landscape evolves and as the software undergoes updates and changes, continuous security testing ensures that the system remains resilient against new and emerging threats. This ongoing vigilance is critical to maintaining the trust of users and stakeholders, safeguarding sensitive data, and ensuring compliance with regulatory requirements.

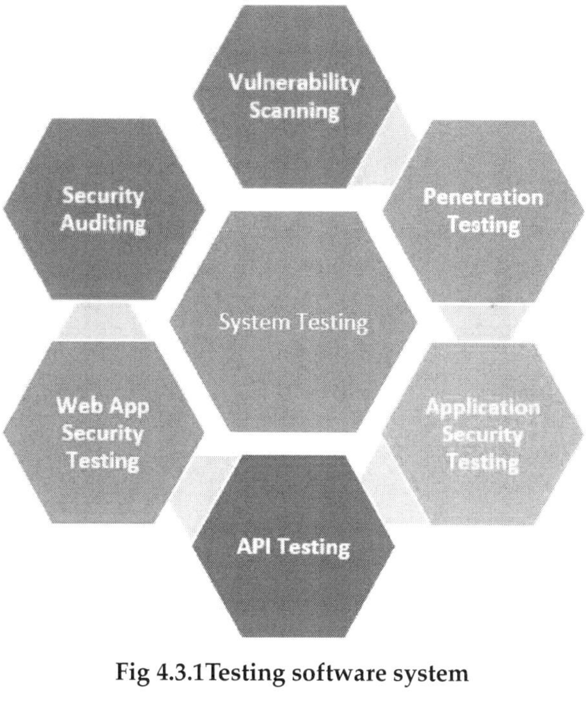

Fig 4.3.1Testing software system

4.4 Using Agile Methods to Improve Software Testing

Using Agile methods to improve software testing fundamentally reshapes how quality assurance is approached, creating a more dynamic, responsive, and integrated process that enhances the overall effectiveness of the development lifecycle. Agile's iterative nature ensures that testing is ongoing, with quality being continuously assessed and improved upon throughout the development process. This approach contrasts sharply with traditional methodologies, where testing often occurs in a distinct phase after development is complete, leading to delays and a higher risk of defects being discovered late in the cycle.

In Agile environments, the role of testers expands beyond merely executing test cases. Testers become active participants in the entire development process, contributing to requirements gathering, user story creation, and the refinement of acceptance criteria. This involvement ensures that testing considerations are incorporated from the very beginning, aligning the development process more closely with user needs and quality objectives. Testers collaborate closely with product owners and developers to ensure that user stories are well-defined and that acceptance criteria are both testable and aligned with the business goals.

Agile emphasizes the importance of automated testing, which plays a crucial role in maintaining the pace and quality of development. Automated tests are developed in parallel with the code, and they are integrated into continuous integration/continuous delivery (CI/CD) pipelines. These pipelines automatically execute the tests each time new code is committed, providing immediate feedback to the developers. This rapid feedback loop is essential in Agile, where teams must quickly identify and resolve defects to maintain momentum and meet sprint goals.

The focus on early and continuous testing in Agile reduces the likelihood of defects making it into the production environment. Techniques like shift-left testing, where testing activities are performed earlier in the development process, ensure that defects are caught and addressed when they are cheaper and easier to fix. This proactive approach helps in reducing the overall cost of quality and accelerates the time to market by minimizing the need for extensive rework.

Agile also encourages the practice of pair testing, where testers and developers work together to test the software. This collaborative approach not only enhances the quality of the tests but also fosters knowledge sharing and mutual understanding between testers and developers. It helps bridge the gap between development and testing, ensuring that the software is developed with a strong focus on quality from the outset.

Another important aspect of Agile testing is continuous customer feedback. Agile teams often involve customers or end-users in the testing process, especially during user acceptance testing (UAT). By frequently delivering working software and gathering feedback, teams can make adjustments and improvements in subsequent iterations, ensuring that the final product better meets user needs. This user-centric approach to testing aligns the development process with the ultimate goal of delivering value to the customer.

Exploratory testing is highly valued in Agile environments because it allows testers to go beyond predefined scripts and discover unexpected issues. In Agile, where requirements can evolve rapidly, exploratory testing is particularly effective at uncovering defects that might not be identified through automated or scripted tests. Testers use their creativity and domain knowledge to explore the software in ways that simulate real-world usage, providing a deeper level of assurance about the software's quality.

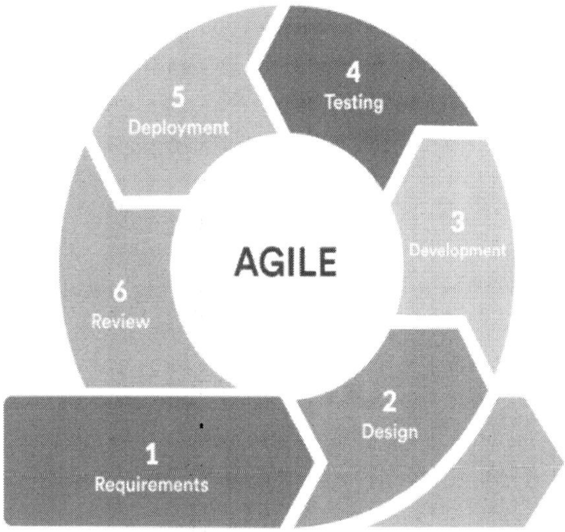

Fig 4.4.1 Agile Methods to Improve Software Testing.

Agile testing also benefits from test metrics and reporting that are tailored to Agile's iterative nature. Metrics such as the number of defects found per sprint, test coverage, and the percentage of automated tests provide valuable insights into the testing process's effectiveness and help teams identify areas for improvement. These metrics are often discussed during sprint retrospectives, where the team reflects on the sprint's successes and challenges. This continuous improvement mindset is a hallmark of Agile, ensuring that the testing process evolves and improves with each iteration.

Agile test management tools are integral to managing the fast-paced and collaborative nature of Agile testing. These tools often integrate seamlessly with other Agile tools, such as issue trackers and version control systems, providing a centralized platform for managing test cases, tracking defects, and reporting on test outcomes. Tools like JIRA, TestRail, and Zephyr are commonly used in Agile environments to streamline test management, enhance visibility, and facilitate communication across the team.

Incorporating Agile methods into software testing also fosters a **culture of quality** within the development team. By embedding testing into every phase of development, Agile encourages all team members, not just testers, to take ownership of the software's quality. This collective responsibility leads to a more thorough and consistent focus on quality, ultimately resulting in a more reliable and user-friendly product.

The flexibility of Agile methods allows testing practices to evolve with the project, adapting to new challenges and changes in requirements. This adaptability is critical in today's fast-paced development environments, where the ability to respond quickly to change can be a significant competitive advantage. By embracing Agile methods in software testing, teams can improve their efficiency, reduce defects, and deliver higher-quality software that better meets the needs of the business and its users.

UNIT 5

TESTING PROCESS AND TOOLS

5.1. Testing Process and Tools

Software testing is an essential part of the software development lifecycle, designed to ensure the quality, functionality, and security of a product before it reaches end-users. It involves systematically identifying and addressing defects in the software through various testing methodologies and tools. The testing process can be categorized into different types, including unit testing, integration testing, system testing, acceptance testing, performance testing, and security testing. Each type serves a specific purpose in validating different aspects of the software.

In the context of modern software development, automated testing has become increasingly important. Selenium, a widely-used open-source tool, is a key player in this field, providing the ability to automate web browser interactions. Selenium supports multiple languages such as Java, Python, and C#, and offers several components, including Selenium IDE, Selenium WebDriver, and Selenium Grid, to cater to different testing needs.

Testing client/server systems, where multiple clients interact with a central server, presents unique challenges, such as ensuring data consistency, handling concurrent users, and maintaining security. Similarly, testing web-based systems requires attention to cross-browser compatibility, responsive design, and security vulnerabilities.

Selenium IDE allows users to create automated test scripts through a simple record-and-playback interface, making it accessible for both beginners and experienced testers. Test scripts can be enhanced with assertions, variables, and XPath for more complex test scenarios. Advanced features like handling dynamic elements, pop-ups, and frames further extend Selenium's capabilities, making it a versatile tool for thorough web application testing.

Effective testing requires a well-organized approach, including managing test suites, reusing code, and integrating with continuous integration tools like Jenkins. By adhering to best practices, such as using the Page Object Model and avoiding hard-coded data, testers can create maintainable, scalable, and efficient automated test cases that contribute significantly to the quality assurance process.

Overall, mastering the testing process and tools like Selenium equips teams to deliver reliable and high-performing software products that meet user needs and withstand the demands of real-world usage.

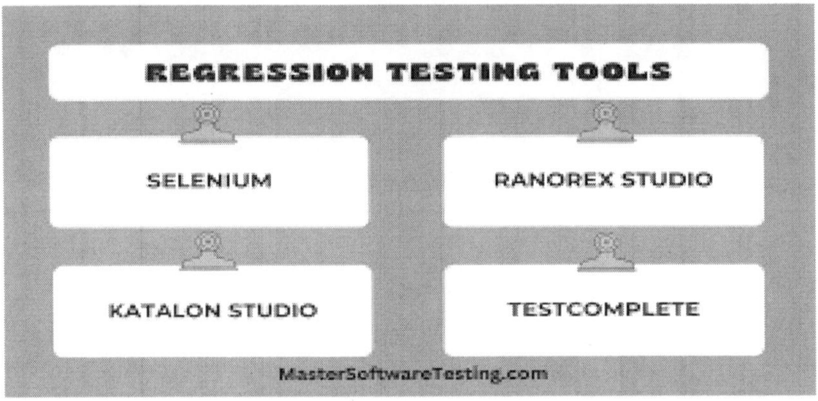

Fig 5.1.1 Testing Tools.

5.2. Testing Client/Server Systems

Testing client/server systems is a comprehensive process crucial for ensuring that applications function reliably, perform efficiently, and remain secure. This architecture involves multiple clients interacting with a centralized server, and effective testing is essential to address the unique challenges of this setup. Here's an in-depth look at how client/server systems work, how to build and test them, and the latest advancements in technology.

1. How Client/Server Systems Work

Client/server systems operate on a network where clients (user devices or applications) request services or data from a server. The server, a central entity, processes these requests and sends back the appropriate responses. This architecture allows for centralized management of data and services, supporting scalability and efficiency.

- Client: The client is the interface through which users interact with the system. It could be a web browser, a desktop application, or a mobile app. The client's role is to send requests to the server and present the server's responses to the user. It handles user input, displays data, and may perform some local processing.

- Server: The server manages data, performs computations, and handles multiple client requests simultaneously. It processes incoming requests, executes the required operations, and returns the results to the clients. The server ensures data consistency, handles authentication, and performs various backend tasks necessary for the application's functionality.

2. Building and Testing Client/Server Systems

Building and testing client/server systems involves several steps to ensure that both components function correctly and work together seamlessly.

2.1 Building Client/Server Systems

- **Design and Architecture:** Define the architecture and design of the system, including the client interface, server functionalities, and network protocols. Choose technologies and frameworks that best fit the system's requirements, such as web technologies for web applications or mobile frameworks for mobile apps.
- **Development:** Develop the client and server components based on the design specifications. Ensure that the client interface is user-friendly and that the server can handle the expected load and process requests efficiently. Implement necessary security measures to protect data and manage user access.
- **Integration:** Integrate the client and server components, ensuring that they communicate effectively. This includes setting up the network infrastructure and configuring any necessary middleware or APIs.

2.2 Testing Client/Server Systems

- **Functional Testing:** Verify that the client and server components function as intended. Test all features and workflows to ensure that user inputs are correctly processed and that the server responds accurately. This includes testing user interactions, data handling, and overall functionality.
- **Performance Testing:** Assess the system's performance under various conditions. Perform load testing to simulate multiple concurrent users and evaluate how the server handles traffic. Conduct stress testing to determine the system's breaking points and scalability testing to ensure it can handle growth.
- **Security Testing:** Test the system for vulnerabilities and ensure that security measures are effective. Check for issues related to authentication, authorization, data encryption, and potential security threats. Use automated tools and manual testing to identify and address vulnerabilities.
- **Usability Testing:** Evaluate the user experience on the client side. Ensure that the client interface is intuitive, easy to navigate, and responsive. Test how the system handles errors and provides feedback to users.

- **Regression Testing:** After updates or changes, re-run tests to ensure that new modifications do not introduce new issues or affect existing functionality. Automated regression testing can help maintain consistency and efficiency.

3. Latest Advancements in Client/Server Technology

The client/server technology landscape is continually evolving, with new advancements enhancing system capabilities and performance.

- **Cloud Computing:** Cloud technologies enable scalable and flexible client/server architectures. Cloud services provide on-demand resources and can handle varying loads efficiently. This allows for improved performance and cost-effectiveness.
- **Micro-services Architecture:** Microservices break down server applications into smaller, independent services that communicate over a network. This architecture improves scalability, maintainability, and deployment flexibility. Each microservice handles a specific function, allowing for easier updates and scaling.
- **Containerization:** Technologies like Docker and Kubernetes facilitate containerization, which packages server applications and their dependencies into portable containers. This approach enhances deployment consistency, scalability, and resource efficiency.
- **Serverless Computing:** Serverless architectures abstract server management tasks, allowing developers to focus on code rather than infrastructure. Serverless platforms automatically scale based on demand and can reduce operational costs.
- **Enhanced Security Measures:** Advances in security technologies, such as advanced encryption techniques, threat detection systems, and AI-driven security solutions, help protect client/server systems from emerging threats and vulnerabilities.
- **Artificial Intelligence and Machine Learning:** AI and ML are increasingly integrated into client/server systems to provide intelligent insights, automate tasks, and enhance user experiences. These technologies can improve decision-making and system efficiency.

5.3. Testing Web-Based Systems with Selenium

Testing web-based systems is a crucial part of software development that ensures web applications function properly across different browsers and devices. This process involves validating the application's performance, usability, and functionality under various conditions. Selenium is a widely used tool for automating web browser interactions, offering a robust framework for testing web-based systems. Selenium's popularity stems from its ability to support multiple programming languages and its flexibility in interacting with various web elements.

Selenium's evolution began with Selenium IDE (Integrated Development Environment), a browser extension designed to simplify the creation of test scripts by recording user interactions. Selenium IDE allows testers to quickly create and execute basic test cases without extensive programming knowledge. However, for more complex scenarios and better control over testing environments, Selenium WebDriver offers a more powerful solution. WebDriver directly interacts with browser elements, providing greater precision and performance compared to Selenium IDE. It supports various programming languages, including Java, Python, C#, and JavaScript, enabling testers to write scripts that can be integrated into existing development workflows and CI/CD pipelines.

One of Selenium WebDriver's key features is its ability to handle cross-browser testing effectively. WebDriver supports a wide range of browsers, including Chrome, Firefox, Safari, and Edge. This feature is essential for ensuring that web applications behave consistently across different browsers and their versions. Additionally, WebDriver's support for advanced locators, such as XPath and CSS Selectors, allows testers to precisely identify and interact with web elements, even in complex and dynamic web pages. This capability is crucial for testing applications with dynamic content and varying element attributes.

In practice, using Selenium involves creating test suites that cover various aspects of the web application. Test suites are collections of test cases designed to validate different functionalities and scenarios. A well-structured test suite includes multiple test cases that address various user interactions and application features. For example, a login test suite might include test cases for successful login, invalid credentials handling, password reset, and logout functionality. Running these test suites helps ensure that all aspects of the application are tested comprehensively, improving the overall quality and reliability of the web application.

Recent advancements in Selenium technology include integration with modern development practices such as continuous integration and continuous delivery (CI/CD). By integrating Selenium tests into CI/CD pipelines, teams can automate the execution of tests as part of the build process, enabling early detection of issues and ensuring that code changes do not introduce new bugs. Additionally, the rise of cloud-based testing platforms and services allows for scalable and efficient test execution across multiple environments, further enhancing the effectiveness of Selenium-based testing strategies.

Overall, Selenium provides a versatile and powerful toolset for testing web-based systems. Its ability to support various programming languages, handle cross-browser testing, and integrate with modern development practices makes it a valuable asset for ensuring the quality and performance of web applications.

As web technologies continue to evolve, Selenium's adaptability and ongoing improvements will continue to play a critical role in the field of web testing.

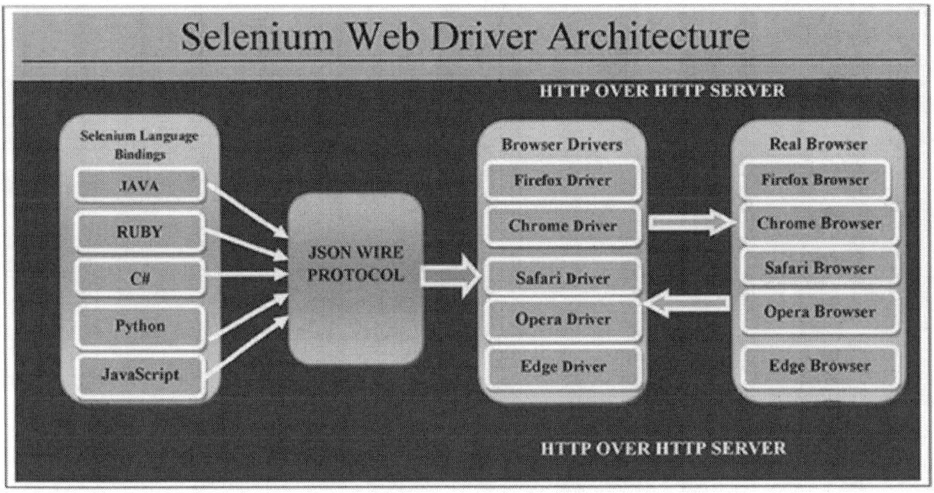

Fig 5.3.1:Selenium Web Driver Architecture.

History of Selenium

Selenium has a rich history that reflects its evolution from a simple script automation tool to a comprehensive suite for browser automation. Here's a detailed look at its development over the years:

1. Early Beginnings: Selenium Core

Selenium was first introduced by Jason Huggins in 2004 as a JavaScript library known as Selenium Core. The primary purpose of Selenium Core was to automate interactions with web applications through a browser, facilitating the testing of web applications' user interfaces. Selenium Core allowed developers to write scripts that could perform various actions, such as clicking buttons and filling out forms, simulating user interactions.

2. Evolution to Selenium Remote Control (RC)

In 2008, Selenium RC (Remote Control) was introduced to address some of the limitations of Selenium Core. Selenium RC enabled the automation of web applications across different browsers by running tests on a server that communicated with the web browser. This new architecture allowed tests to be written in multiple programming languages, such as Java, C#, and Python, and provided greater flexibility in automating web interactions. Selenium RC could interact with browsers through an intermediary server, making it possible to execute test scripts on different browsers and platforms.

3. Introduction of Selenium WebDriver

The next major milestone in Selenium's history was the introduction of Selenium WebDriver in 2009. Selenium WebDriver was developed to overcome the performance and reliability issues associated with Selenium RC. Unlike Selenium RC, which relied on an intermediary server, WebDriver interacts directly with the browser's native API, offering more precise control and faster execution of tests. WebDriver supports multiple programming languages, including Java, C#, Python, and JavaScript, and provides advanced features for interacting with web elements.

4. Selenium Grid for Parallel Testing

In conjunction with Selenium WebDriver, Selenium Grid was introduced to support parallel test execution. Selenium Grid allows for the distribution of test cases across multiple machines and browsers, enabling the simultaneous execution of tests and significantly reducing test execution time. This capability is particularly useful for cross-browser testing and scaling test operations, making it easier to verify that web applications work correctly across different environments.

5. Continuous Integration and Cloud Testing

In recent years, Selenium has increasingly integrated with modern development practices, including continuous integration (CI) and continuous delivery (CD) pipelines. By integrating Selenium tests into CI/CD workflows, teams can automate the execution of tests as part of the development process, catching issues early and ensuring that code changes do not introduce new bugs. Additionally, the rise of cloud-based testing platforms has enhanced Selenium's capabilities by providing scalable environments for running tests across multiple browsers and devices, further improving testing efficiency and coverage.

6. Ongoing Development and Community Contributions

Selenium continues to evolve through contributions from the open-source community and ongoing development efforts. New versions of Selenium are released regularly, introducing enhancements and support for emerging web technologies. The Selenium project is maintained by a dedicated team of contributors and developers who work to address bugs, improve performance, and incorporate new features based on user feedback and industry trends.

In summary, Selenium's history reflects its growth from a basic automation tool to a sophisticated framework that supports comprehensive web testing. Its evolution has been driven by the need for more efficient, flexible, and scalable testing solutions, making it a crucial tool for ensuring the quality of web applications in an ever-changing technological landscape.

5.4.Selenium IDE: Full Definition and Overview

Selenium IDE (Integrated Development Environment) is a browser extension designed to facilitate the creation and execution of automated test scripts for web applications. It serves as a valuable tool for testers who need to quickly develop and manage test cases without requiring extensive programming knowledge. Available as an extension for both Firefox and Chrome browsers, Selenium IDE provides a user-friendly interface that simplifies the process of recording, editing, and executing tests.

Selenium IDE operates by recording user interactions with a web application, such as clicks, form entries, and navigation actions. When a user engages with a web page, Selenium IDE captures these actions and translates them into a series of commands that are stored in a test script. This feature allows testers to generate test cases quickly by simply performing the desired actions in the browser. Once recorded, these test scripts can be edited to refine test scenarios, add assertions, or modify commands as needed.

The IDE supports a range of commands for automating various aspects of web testing. Key commands include open, which navigates to a specified URL; type, which inputs text into a form field; click, which simulates mouse clicks on elements; and assertText, which verifies that a particular text appears on the page. These commands can be combined to create comprehensive test scenarios that validate different functionalities of the web application.

In addition to recording and executing tests, Selenium IDE provides features for debugging and maintaining test scripts. Testers can use breakpoints to pause execution at specific points, allowing for detailed examination of the test's behavior and the web application's state. This capability helps identify and resolve issues during test development. The IDE also offers options to export test cases to various programming languages, such as Java, Python, and JavaScript, which can be utilized for more advanced test automation using Selenium WebDriver.

Selenium IDE includes a set of tools for locating web elements on a page, which is crucial for creating reliable and accurate test scripts. It supports multiple locator strategies, including ID, class name, name, link text, XPath, and CSS selectors. Testers can use these locators to identify elements with specific attributes, ensuring that the test scripts interact with the correct components on the web page.

Despite its ease of use and convenience, Selenium IDE has limitations compared to Selenium WebDriver. While it is suitable for creating simple test cases and prototypes, it lacks the advanced features and flexibility offered by WebDriver. Selenium IDE may struggle with dynamic web elements or complex scenarios that require sophisticated interactions. However, it remains a valuable tool for initial test development and for users who need to quickly automate basic web interactions.

Overall, Selenium IDE provides a straightforward and accessible means of creating automated tests for web applications. Its record-and-playback functionality, coupled with basic editing and debugging features, makes it an ideal starting point for those new to test automation. For more complex testing needs, Selenium IDE can be integrated with Selenium WebDriver, enabling a seamless transition from simple test scenarios to more advanced automation frameworks.

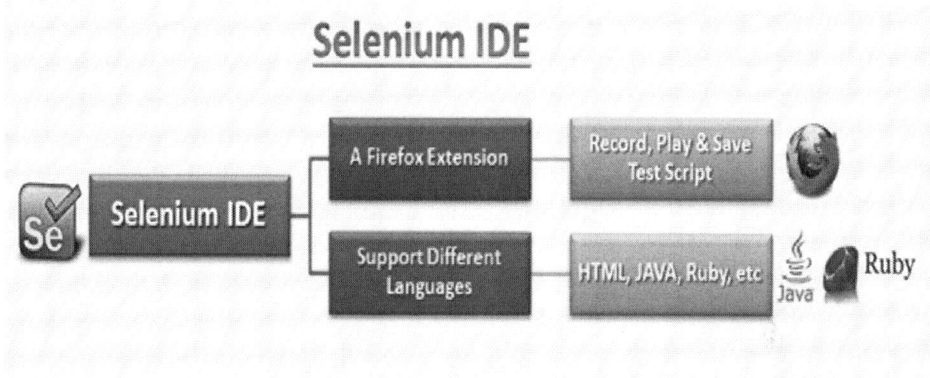

Fig 5.5.1 Selenium IDE.

5.5.Basic IDE Script in Selenium: Full Definition

A basic IDE script in Selenium refers to a test script created using Selenium IDE (Integrated Development Environment), which is a tool designed for recording and automating web interactions through a browser extension. Selenium IDE is particularly useful for users who want to quickly develop and execute test cases without requiring extensive programming skills. The IDE allows users to record their interactions with a web application and then generate a script that can be replayed to automate those interactions. These scripts are essential for validating the functionality of web applications and ensuring they behave as expected under various conditions.

1. Recording a Basic IDE Script:

To create a basic IDE script, a user starts by launching the Selenium IDE extension in a web browser, such as Firefox or Chrome. Once the IDE is open, users begin recording their interactions with the web application they wish to test. As the user navigates through the application, performs actions like clicking buttons, entering data into forms, or selecting items from menus, Selenium IDE captures these interactions and converts them into a series of commands in the script. This recorded script reflects the sequence of actions performed by the user and can be used to replicate the test scenario automatically.

2. Components of a Basic IDE Script:

A basic IDE script consists of several key components:

- **Commands:** Each command in the script represents a specific action or assertion. Common commands include open (to navigate to a URL), type (to enter text into a field), click (to simulate mouse clicks), and assertText (to verify the presence of specific text on the page). Commands are executed in the order they appear in the script.
- **Target:** The target specifies the web element that the command will interact with. For example, when using the click command, the target might be a button's ID or a link's text. The target helps Selenium IDE identify which element on the page the command should affect.
- **Value:** The value component is used to provide additional information for certain commands. For instance, when using the type command, the value specifies the text to be entered into a form field. This component is essential for commands that require input or specific parameters.

3. Editing and Enhancing the Script:

After recording a basic script, users can enhance it by editing the commands, targets, and values to tailor the test scenarios to their needs. Selenium IDE provides a user-friendly interface for making these adjustments. Users can modify existing commands, add new ones, and organize them into test suites for better management. Additionally, Selenium IDE allows for the inclusion of assertions and verification steps to ensure that the web application behaves correctly.

4. Executing and Debugging the Script:

Once the basic IDE script is created and refined, it can be executed to perform the automated test. Selenium IDE provides options to run the script in real-time, allowing users to observe the automated interactions with the web application. During execution, users can monitor the script's progress and identify any issues or failures. Selenium IDE also includes debugging features, such as setting breakpoints and pausing execution, to facilitate the troubleshooting of test scripts.

5. Exporting Scripts:

For users who require more advanced testing capabilities, Selenium IDE allows for the export of scripts to various programming languages, such as Java, Python, and JavaScript. Exporting scripts enables integration with Selenium WebDriver, providing a pathway to more sophisticated test automation frameworks. This feature is particularly useful for scaling test automation efforts and incorporating tests into continuous integration and delivery (CI/CD) pipelines.

5.6. XPath Finder: Full Definition

XPath, or XML Path Language, is a versatile query language utilized for navigating and selecting nodes within XML and HTML documents. In the context of web testing and automation, XPath plays a crucial role in locating and interacting with specific elements on a web page. An XPath finder is a tool or feature that aids in the creation and validation of XPath expressions, which are used to identify elements with precision, ensuring effective test automation.

XPath's syntax and structure are foundational to its use. It employs a combination of nodes, axes, predicates, and functions to create queries that traverse the document's hierarchy. Nodes represent various parts of the document, such as elements and attributes, while axes define the relationships between these nodes, such as child, parent, or descendant. Predicates, enclosed in square brackets, filter nodes based on specific criteria, like [1] for the first element or [contains(@ attribute, 'value')] for elements with certain attributes. XPath functions, such as contains() or text(), further refine these queries by performing operations on the selected nodes.

An XPath finder is designed to simplify the process of crafting XPath expressions. Often integrated into browser developer tools or provided as standalone utilities, XPath finders offer several key functionalities. They allow users to inspect and interact with elements on a web page, generating XPath expressions based on the element's attributes and structure. This process involves selecting an element, after which the finder produces an XPath query that reflects the element's location and characteristics. Additionally, XPath finders include validation tools that enable users to test whether their XPath expressions accurately locate the intended elements, ensuring reliability before incorporating them into automated test scripts.

For practical use, XPath finders enhance efficiency by enabling quick generation and testing of XPath expressions. Users can inspect elements in real-time, generate preliminary XPath queries, and validate these queries to confirm their accuracy. This capability is essential for creating robust test automation scripts that interact correctly with web elements, even when page structures are complex or dynamic.

When employing XPath, best practices should be followed to ensure effectiveness and maintainability. Avoid overly complex or absolute paths that are prone to breakage if the page structure changes. Instead, use relative paths and unique identifiers when available. Regularly validate and test XPath expressions to verify their functionality and adapt them as needed to accommodate changes in the web application.

In advanced scenarios, XPath's ability to handle dynamic content and combine multiple conditions allows for more sophisticated queries. Functions like contains() help manage dynamic attributes, while combined predicates refine selections further. Incorporating XPath into automation frameworks, such as Selenium, allows testers to leverage these expressions for various actions, from clicking buttons to verifying text.

Overall, XPath finders are indispensable tools in web testing, providing a means to create, test, and refine XPath expressions effectively. Their integration into testing workflows and their support for XPath's powerful querying capabilities make them essential for maintaining high-quality web applications through automated testing.

XPath, or XML Path Language, is a crucial technology used in web automation for selecting and interacting with elements within XML and HTML documents. XPath provides a method to navigate through the hierarchical structure of these documents, enabling precise identification of elements based on their attributes, content, and position. An XPath finder is an indispensable tool that facilitates the creation and validation of XPath expressions, which are essential for automating interactions with web elements in various testing frameworks, such as Selenium.

The core functionality of XPath revolves around its syntax, which includes nodes, axes, predicates, and functions. Nodes are the fundamental components of XPath queries, representing elements, attributes, text, and other parts of the document. Axes define the relationships and direction of navigation between nodes, such as child for selecting direct children, parent for selecting the parent node, descendant for selecting all descendants, and ancestor for selecting all ancestors. Predicates, enclosed in square brackets, filter nodes based on specific conditions, allowing users to refine their queries. For example, [1] targets the first node, while [contains(@attribute, 'value')] selects nodes where an attribute contains a specific value. XPath functions like contains(), starts-with(), and text() enhance querying by performing operations on node attributes and text content.

XPath finders are tools designed to simplify the process of generating and validating XPath expressions. These tools are often integrated into browser developer tools or provided as standalone applications. They allow users to inspect web elements interactively, generating XPath expressions based on the selected elements' attributes and structure. This functionality helps users quickly obtain XPath queries, which can then be refined to suit specific testing needs. Additionally, XPath finders offer validation features, enabling users to test whether their XPath expressions accurately locate the intended elements. This validation process ensures that the expressions are reliable and effective before being incorporated into automated test scripts.

In practical terms, XPath finders enhance the efficiency of developing and managing automated tests for web applications. By enabling quick generation and testing of XPath expressions, these tools streamline the process of creating robust test automation scripts. Best practices for using XPath include preferring relative paths over absolute ones to maintain flexibility and avoiding overly complex queries that may break with changes in the document structure. Whenever possible, using unique attributes such as id or name provides a more reliable way to locate elements. Regular validation and testing of XPath expressions are essential to ensure their accuracy and adapt them to changes in the web application.

Advanced XPath techniques include combining multiple conditions within a single query to create precise selections, handling dynamic content using functions like contains() and starts-with(), and integrating XPath expressions into automation frameworks for programmatic interaction with web elements. By following these practices and leveraging the capabilities of XPath finders, testers can develop effective and maintainable automated tests, ensuring the quality and functionality of web applications. The ongoing evolution of web technologies and testing frameworks continues to enhance the relevance and utility of XPath in test automation, making it a fundamental tool for ensuring robust and reliable web-based testing.

5.7. Basic Test Suites: Comprehensive Overview

Basic test suites are integral to the software testing process, offering a structured and organized approach to evaluating specific aspects of a software application. They play a critical role in ensuring that software functions correctly, meets its requirements, and performs reliably under various conditions. By grouping together related test cases, test suites facilitate systematic testing, enabling testers to validate the application's behavior comprehensively.

A basic test suite is essentially a collection of test cases designed to assess various functionalities or features of a software application. Each test case within the suite is crafted to evaluate a specific aspect of the application, such as a particular function or feature. The core components of a basic test suite include test cases, test data, expected results, and an execution order. Test cases are the individual tests that outline the steps to be executed, the input data required, and the expected outcomes. They provide a detailed guide for testers to follow, ensuring that each aspect of the application is thoroughly evaluated.

Test data is another critical component of a basic test suite. It represents the input information used during test execution and is essential for simulating different scenarios that the application might encounter. Proper test data helps ensure that the application is tested under various conditions, including edge cases and unusual inputs. Expected results define what the application should produce or how it should behave if the test case passes. By comparing actual results with these expected outcomes, testers can determine whether the application is functioning correctly.

The execution order of test cases within a test suite can vary depending on the dependencies between tests. Some test suites may specify a particular order in which test cases should be executed, especially if there are setup steps or interdependencies between tests. This organized approach ensures that the testing process is systematic and that all required conditions are met before executing certain test cases.

Creating a basic test suite involves several key steps. First, testers need to define the test objectives by identifying the features or functionalities that require testing. This involves understanding the application's requirements and determining which aspects are critical for validation. Next, testers design test cases that cover various scenarios, including both typical and edge cases. Each test case should be detailed, with clear instructions for execution and specific criteria for success.

Once test cases are designed, they are organized into a test suite. Grouping related test cases helps streamline the testing process, making it easier to manage and execute tests systematically. Test data is then prepared to ensure that all necessary inputs are available for executing the test cases. Defining expected results is crucial for evaluating the application's behavior and determining whether it meets the specified requirements.

After creating the test suite, testers execute the test cases according to the defined order or independently, depending on their dependencies. Results are recorded, and any issues or defects encountered are documented. This process is followed by a review of the test results to identify patterns or recurring issues. The test suite may be refined based on the findings, addressing any gaps or updating it to reflect changes in the application.

Basic test suites can be categorized into different types based on their focus and purpose. A functional test suite verifies that specific functions or features of the application work as intended. It ensures that each functionality performs correctly according to the specified requirements. A regression test suite is designed to verify that recent changes or updates have not introduced new defects or caused existing features to fail. Smoke test suites, also known as build verification test suites, consist of preliminary tests that check the basic functionality of the application before more detailed testing is performed. Integration test suites focus on testing the interactions between different components or systems to ensure they work together as expected.

The benefits of using basic test suites are numerous. They provide comprehensive coverage by grouping related test cases, ensuring that all critical aspects of the application are tested. This organized approach enhances efficiency, making it easier to manage and execute tests systematically. Consistency in testing is achieved through the structured approach provided by test suites, reducing the risk of missing important tests. Additionally, basic test suites facilitate the early identification of defects and issues by systematically evaluating various scenarios and comparing actual results with expected outcomes.

In conclusion, basic test suites are essential tools in the software testing process, offering a structured and organized approach to evaluating an application's functionality. By grouping related test cases, preparing necessary test data, and defining expected results, test suites help ensure comprehensive, efficient, and consistent testing. They play a vital role in validating software functionality, identifying defects, and maintaining overall software quality, making them indispensable in the pursuit of high-quality software development.

5.8. Locator Types: ID, ClassName, Name, Link Text, XPath

In the realm of web automation and testing, effective interaction with web elements is crucial. This interaction is facilitated by locators, which are strategies or methods used to identify and interact with elements on a web page. Different locator types serve distinct purposes, each with its strengths and limitations. Understanding these locator types—ID, ClassName, Name, Link Text, and XPath—is essential for developing robust and efficient automation scripts. This comprehensive exploration delves into each locator type, their characteristics, and their practical applications in web testing.

5.9. ID Locator

The ID locator is one of the most commonly used and reliable methods for identifying web elements. It leverages the unique identifier assigned to each element in the HTML document through the id attribute. The primary advantage of using IDs is their uniqueness; each ID value should be unique within the scope of a single HTML document. This uniqueness allows for precise targeting of elements, minimizing the risk of ambiguity and improving the accuracy of test scripts. The syntax for using an ID locator in many automation tools is straightforward. For instance, in Selenium WebDriver, the ID locator is utilized with the By.id() method. The efficiency of the ID locator is attributed to its direct access to elements based on their unique attributes, making it ideal for locating elements that are consistently present on a web page.

However, the effectiveness of the ID locator depends on the proper implementation of unique IDs in the HTML. In cases where IDs are not unique or are dynamically generated, the locator may fail to find the intended element. Despite this limitation, the ID locator remains a preferred choice for its simplicity and reliability when used with properly defined unique identifiers.

5.10. ClassName Locator

The ClassName locator identifies elements based on the class attribute assigned to them in the HTML document. The class attribute can be used to apply styles to multiple elements, and it can also serve as a means to group elements with similar characteristics. In automation tools like Selenium WebDriver, the By.className() method is employed to locate elements using their class names. One of the advantages of the ClassName locator is its ability to select multiple elements that share the same class, making it useful for scenarios where elements are grouped by a common style or functionality.

Despite its advantages, the ClassName locator has limitations. Since class names are not unique, this locator may select multiple elements if they share the same class attribute. This can be problematic when precise targeting is required, as the locator might return a collection of elements rather than a single, specific element. To mitigate this issue, it is essential to ensure that class names are used strategically and in conjunction with other locators when necessary to achieve accurate results.

5.11. Name Locator

The Name locator identifies elements using the name attribute in the HTML document. This attribute is often used in forms to name input fields and other elements. In Selenium WebDriver, the By.name() method is used to locate elements based on their name attribute. The Name locator is particularly useful for targeting form elements and is effective in scenarios where the name attribute is consistently applied.

However, similar to the ClassName locator, the Name locator may encounter challenges if multiple elements share the same name attribute. This can lead to ambiguity and may require additional locators to refine the selection. Despite this, the Name locator remains a valuable tool for accessing form elements and other elements with distinct naming conventions.

5.12. Link Text Locator

The Link Text locator is specifically designed for identifying anchor elements (<a>) that contain hyperlinks. It utilizes the text contained within the anchor tags to locate elements. In Selenium WebDriver, the By.linkText() method is employed for this purpose. The primary advantage of the Link Text locator is its ability to directly target links based on their visible text, making it useful for interactions involving navigation or hyperlink verification.

The Link Text locator requires an exact match of the link text, which means that any changes to the visible text will necessitate updates to the locator. Additionally, if multiple links have the same text, this locator may select the wrong element. To address these issues, variations of the Link Text locator, such as PartialLinkText, allow for partial matching of link text, providing more flexibility in identifying elements with similar but not identical text.

5.13. XPath Locator

XPath (XML Path Language) is a powerful query language used for locating elements within XML and HTML documents. It allows for precise targeting of elements based on various attributes, relationships, and content. XPath locators can navigate through the hierarchical structure of a document, making them highly versatile and capable of addressing complex scenarios. In Selenium WebDriver, the By.xpath() method is used to implement XPath locators.

XPath provides a rich set of features, including the ability to use functions, predicates, and axes to construct detailed queries. For example, XPath expressions can select elements based on attribute values, text content, or hierarchical relationships. The flexibility of XPath allows for the creation of highly specific queries that can handle dynamic and complex page structures. However, XPath expressions can become intricate and may impact performance if not optimized correctly.

Despite its power, XPath requires a thorough understanding of its syntax and capabilities to be used effectively. Complex XPath expressions can be harder to maintain and debug, especially if they rely on fragile or dynamic attributes. It is essential to balance the use of XPath with other locator types and to ensure that expressions are crafted to be robust and efficient.

5.14. CSS Selector: In-Depth Explanation

CSS selectors are a cornerstone of web automation and testing, providing a powerful means to identify and interact with elements on a web page. Originally designed for styling purposes in Cascading Style Sheets, CSS selectors have proven invaluable in the context of web testing due to their versatility and efficiency. Understanding CSS selectors involves grasping their various types and functionalities, which enable precise targeting of web elements based on attributes, types, states, and hierarchical relationships.

CSS selectors come in several types, each serving distinct purposes. The **Type Selector** targets all elements of a specified type, such as div for all <div> elements or p for all <p> elements. This selector is straightforward and useful for applying styles to elements of a particular type, making it one of the simplest methods for element selection. The **Class Selector**, denoted by a period followed by the class name (e.g., .button), selects elements based on their class attribute. It allows for the grouping of elements with shared styles or functionalities, which is beneficial for targeting multiple elements with similar characteristics.

The **ID Selector**, identified by a hash symbol followed by the ID (e.g., #header), is designed to select a unique element based on its ID attribute. Since IDs are meant to be unique within an HTML document, this selector provides a precise means of targeting a single element. However, the effectiveness of the ID Selector relies on the proper assignment of unique IDs. The **Attribute Selector** targets elements based on the presence or value of an attribute. It can be used in various forms, such as [type="text"] to select elements with a specific attribute value. This selector offers flexibility for identifying elements with particular attributes and is especially useful for forms and interactive elements.

The **Descendant Selector** selects elements that are descendants of a specified element, using a space to separate the ancestor from the descendant (e.g., div p selects all <p> elements inside <div> elements). This selector is valuable for targeting elements within a specific section of a page. The **Child Selector** targets elements that are direct children of a specified element, using a greater-than symbol (e.g., ul> li selects <li> elements that are direct children of a <ul>). This selector is useful for targeting elements that are immediate children, ensuring precise control over element selection.

Sibling Selectors are used to target elements based on their position relative to other elements. The **Adjacent Sibling Selector** (e.g., h1 + p) selects the first <p> element that immediately follows an <h1>, while the **General Sibling Selector** (e.g., h1 ~ p) selects all <p> elements that are siblings of an <h1>. These selectors are useful for selecting elements based on their relationship to preceding or sibling elements.

Pseudo-Class Selectors target elements based on their state or position. For instance, a:hover selects links when hovered over by the cursor, and :first-child targets the first child of a parent element. These selectors are beneficial for applying styles based on user interactions or element positions. **Pseudo-Element Selectors** like p::first-line target specific parts of an element or virtual elements not present in the DOM, allowing for styling of particular parts of content.

CSS selectors offer several advantages in web automation. They provide a simple and readable syntax, making test scripts easier to write and maintain. Additionally, CSS selectors are generally efficient, as they are natively supported by browsers and can offer better performance compared to complex XPath expressions. Their flexibility allows for precise targeting through various combinations of selectors, and they are often more maintainable than XPath when dealing with dynamic content.

In conclusion, CSS selectors are a fundamental tool for web automation, offering a robust and flexible method for identifying and interacting with web elements. By understanding and utilizing different types of CSS selectors, testers and developers can effectively target elements based on their attributes, types, states, and relationships, leading to more efficient and reliable web testing. The combination of simplicity, performance, and versatility makes CSS selectors a key component in the toolkit of anyone involved in web development and testing.

5.15. Locating Elements in a Browser: Overview of Selenium WebDriver and Case Study

Locating elements in a browser is a crucial aspect of web automation testing, especially when using tools like Selenium WebDriver. Selenium WebDriver is a powerful open-source framework that allows testers to automate interactions with web browsers, simulating user actions to validate the functionality and performance of web applications. A key component of this process is the ability to accurately identify and interact with web elements—such as buttons, forms, and links—based on their attributes and hierarchical relationships within the HTML structure.

Selenium WebDriver supports various methods for locating elements, each tailored to different scenarios. For instance, the **ID locator** is used to select elements with a unique id attribute, offering a fast and reliable way to target specific elements. Similarly, the **ClassName locator** allows testers to find elements based on their class attributes, which is particularly useful when multiple elements share the same styling or behavior. The **Name locator** targets elements by their name attribute, often employed for form fields, while the **LinkText locator** and **PartialLinkText locator** are designed to identify hyperlinks based on their visible text, either fully or partially.

For more complex scenarios, Selenium WebDriver provides the **XPath locator**, which uses XPath expressions to navigate through the HTML structure and select elements based on a wide range of criteria, including their attributes, positions, or content. Similarly, the **CSS Selector** is another versatile method that leverages CSS selectors to locate elements based on their styling information, such as class, ID, or even pseudo-classes. CSS Selectors are often preferred for their efficiency and performance, especially when dealing with dynamic web pages.

To illustrate the practical use of these locators, consider a case study where the goal is to automate the login process for a web application and verify that the user is redirected to a dashboard page upon successful login. In this scenario, Selenium WebDriver can be used to locate the username and password fields by their IDs, fill in the required credentials, and then click the login button identified by its class name. After the login action is performed, WebDriver can verify the success of the operation by checking for a specific element on the dashboard, such as a welcome message located using an XPath expression.

This process highlights the versatility and effectiveness of Selenium WebDriver in automating web testing tasks. By understanding and effectively using the various locator strategies, testers can ensure that their automated scripts are robust, maintainable, and capable of accurately interacting with the web application's elements, thereby improving the overall quality and reliability of the software.

5.16. Locating Elements in a Browser: Overview of Selenium WebDriver

Locating elements within a web browser is one of the most fundamental tasks in web automation testing. This process is essential for interacting with the web page elements and performing various actions, such as clicking buttons, entering text in input fields, and extracting data for validation. Selenium WebDriver is a widely adopted tool for automating web browsers, and it offers a robust set of capabilities for locating and interacting with elements in a web page.

Selenium WebDriver was developed as a successor to Selenium RC (Remote Control) and provides a more direct and user-friendly way of interacting with web browsers. It allows for cross-browser testing by supporting multiple web browsers like Google Chrome, Mozilla Firefox, Internet Explorer, and more. WebDriver works by sending commands to the browser using its native support for automation, making it faster and more reliable compared to its predecessor.

Understanding Selenium WebDriver

Selenium WebDriver operates by launching a browser instance and then sending commands to the browser to perform specific actions, such as navigating to a URL, clicking a button, or retrieving the text from a webpage. The ability to automate these tasks makes WebDriver a powerful tool for testing web applications, as it enables the simulation of user interactions without manual intervention.

One of the core features of WebDriver is its ability to locate elements on a webpage. The process of locating elements is crucial because it determines how the WebDriver interacts with the webpage. Elements can be anything from buttons, text boxes, and links to more complex items like drop-down menus and dynamic elements that appear after some user interaction. WebDriver provides several methods for locating these elements, and choosing the correct locator strategy is key to building efficient and reliable tests.

Locator Strategies in Selenium WebDriver

WebDriver provides a variety of locator strategies, each designed to identify elements based on different attributes or relationships within the HTML document. These locator strategies include By ID, By Name, By Class Name, By Tag Name, By Link Text, By Partial Link Text, By XPath, and By CSS Selector. Each of these strategies has its strengths and ideal use cases, making them suitable for different scenarios encountered during web automation.

By ID: The ID locator is one of the most commonly used strategies for finding elements because an ID is supposed to be unique within an HTML document. Using the ID locator is straightforward and efficient, as it provides a direct reference to the element. For example, if a login button has the ID loginBtn, it can be located with the command driver.findElement(By.id("loginBtn")). This method is not only quick but also ensures that the element is uniquely identified, reducing the risk of interacting with the wrong element.

By Name: The Name locator works similarly to the ID locator but targets the name attribute of elements. This method is especially useful for form elements where the name attribute is commonly used. For instance, an input field for the username with the name username can be located with driver.findElement(By.name("username")). However, unlike IDs, names may not be unique across the document, so extra caution is required when using this locator strategy.

By Class Name: The Class Name locator identifies elements based on their class attribute. This is particularly useful when you want to apply a test action to all elements of a particular class or when a specific element's functionality is tied to its class. For example, if multiple buttons share the class submitBtn, they can all be selected with driver.findElements(By.className("submitBtn")). However, this method can also lead to less specificity if multiple elements share the same class, so it may require additional filtering.

By Tag Name: The Tag Name locator is used to find elements by their HTML tag, such as div, p, or input. This locator is useful when you need to target all elements of a certain type within a specific context. For example, to find all input elements on a page, you could use driver.findElements(By.tagName("input")). While this locator is helpful in certain situations, it is often too broad for precise element targeting.

By Link Text: The Link Text locator identifies anchor elements (<a>) based on the visible text they display. This is particularly useful for navigation links. For example, a link with the text Home can be located with driver.findElement(By.linkText("Home")). However, this locator requires an exact match of the text, which can be limiting if the text changes dynamically or includes extra spaces.

By Partial Link Text: The Partial Link Text locator is similar to the Link Text locator but allows for partial matching of the text. This method is useful when you know only a portion of the link text or when the full text might change. For instance, if the full text of a link is Click here to continue, you could locate it using driver.findElement(By.partialLinkText("Click here")). This method offers more flexibility compared to the Link Text locator but still relies on the accuracy of the partial text.

By XPath: XPath is a powerful and flexible language used to navigate through elements and attributes in an XML document, and by extension, in an HTML document. The XPath locator in WebDriver allows for complex queries that can target elements based on a wide range of criteria, including their attributes, positions, and hierarchical relationships within the DOM. For example, an input element with a specific class inside a form can be located with driver.findElement(By.xpath("//form//input[@class='form-control']")). XPath is particularly useful for targeting elements in dynamic or complex web pages where other locators might fall short.

By CSS Selector: CSS Selectors are used primarily for styling elements on a webpage, but they are also incredibly useful for locating elements in Selenium WebDriver. CSS Selectors allow for precise targeting of elements based on their attributes, class, ID, and even pseudo-classes. For instance, an element with the class login-input that is a child of a div can be selected with driver.findElement(By.cssSelector("div .login-input")). CSS Selectors are often faster than XPath and provide a clean, readable syntax, making them a popular choice among testers.

5.17. Practical Applications: Case Study

To better understand how these locator strategies are used in practice, consider a case study involving the automation of a login process for a web application. The goal of this case study is to automate the steps involved in logging into the application and verifying that the user is redirected to the correct page after a successful login.

Scenario: The web application features a login page where users must enter their username and password to access the dashboard. The dashboard displays a welcome message upon successful login, and the task is to automate this process using Selenium WebDriver.

Step 1: Setting Up the Test Environment

The first step in automating the login process is to set up the test environment. This involves initializing the WebDriver instance and navigating to the login page of the web application. Depending on the browser you are testing, you would initiate the appropriate WebDriver, such as ChromeDriver for Google Chrome or GeckoDriver for Firefox.

java

Copy code

```
WebDriver driver = new ChromeDriver();
driver.get("http://example.com/login");
```

Step 2: Locating the Username and Password Fields

Once the browser is navigated to the login page, the next step is to locate the username and password input fields. Suppose the username field has an ID of username and the password field has an ID of password. These elements can be located using the By ID locator.

java

Copy code

```
WebElementusernameField = driver.findElement(By.id("username"));
WebElementpasswordField = driver.findElement(By.id("password"));
```

Step 3: Entering Credentials

After locating the input fields, the test script needs to enter valid credentials. This is done by using the sendKeys() method to simulate typing into the input fields.

java

Copy code

```
usernameField.sendKeys("testuser");
passwordField.sendKeys("password123");
```

Step 4: Locating and Clicking the Login Button

Next, the login button must be located and clicked to submit the form. Suppose the login button has a class name login-btn. It can be located using the By ClassName locator, and then the click() method can be used to simulate the click action.

```
java
Copy code
WebElementloginButton = driver.findElement(By.className("login-btn"));
loginButton.click();
```

Step 5: Verifying the Login

Once the login button is clicked, the test script should verify whether the login was successful by checking for the presence of a specific element on the dashboard page. For example, a welcome message with the text Welcome might indicate a successful login. This can be done using the By XPath locator.

```
java
Copy code
WebElementwelcomeMessage = driver.findElement(By.xpath("//
h1[text()='Welcome']"));
assertTrue(welcomeMessage.isDisplayed());
```

Step 6: Cleaning Up

Finally, after completing the test, the WebDriver instance should be closed to end the session.

```
java
Copy code
driver.quit();
```

5.18. Using Selenium IDE: Writing a Test Suite Containing a Minimum of 4 Test Cases

Selenium IDE (Integrated Development Environment) is one of the most user-friendly tools in the Selenium suite, designed to simplify the process of creating automated tests for web applications. Unlike Selenium WebDriver, which requires programming knowledge to write scripts, Selenium IDE offers a graphical interface that allows users to record, edit, and play back test scripts without needing to write any code. This makes it an excellent choice for beginners or for teams looking to quickly generate test cases without the overhead of coding.

Selenium IDE was initially created as a Firefox add-on, allowing users to record their interactions with web applications directly in the browser. With advancements in web technology, Selenium IDE has evolved and is now available as a browser extension for both Firefox and Chrome, making it accessible to a broader audience. It supports the creation of test suites, which are collections of test cases that can be run together, providing comprehensive coverage for the application under test.

Getting Started with Selenium IDE

Before diving into writing a test suite, it's essential to understand the basic features of Selenium IDE and how it operates. Selenium IDE works by recording user actions in the browser, such as clicks, typing, and navigation. These actions are recorded as commands in a script, which can be played back to simulate the same interactions. The recorded scripts can be edited to add conditions, loops, or assertions, making them more robust and adaptable to different testing scenarios.

To start using Selenium IDE, you first need to install the browser extension. Once installed, you can launch Selenium IDE from the browser's toolbar, where you'll be greeted with the option to start recording a new test or open an existing project. For this example, we'll create a new test suite from scratch, focusing on a simple web application with a login feature, navigation to a dashboard, and a few interactive elements.

Writing a Test Suite: Case Study

Let's consider a case study where the objective is to create a test suite for a web application that includes the following features:

1. **Login Functionality:** The application requires users to log in with a username and password.
2. **Dashboard Navigation:** Upon successful login, users are redirected to a dashboard.
3. **Form Submission:** The dashboard contains a form that users must fill out and submit.
4. **Logout Functionality:** After completing the form, users can log out of the application.

We will create a test suite in Selenium IDE that covers these four scenarios, ensuring that each aspect of the application's functionality is tested.

Test Case 1: Login Functionality

The first test case in our suite will focus on testing the login functionality of the application. The objective is to verify that users can successfully log in using valid credentials and that they are redirected to the appropriate page after logging in.

Step 1: Start Recording the Test Case

- Open Selenium IDE and start a new recording.
- Navigate to the login page of the web application.

Step 2: Record User Actions

- In the username field, type the test username (e.g., testuser).
- In the password field, type the test password (e.g., password123).
- Click the "Login" button to submit the form.

Step 3: Verify the Outcome

- After the login button is clicked, the application should redirect to the dashboard. Record an assertion to verify that the dashboard page is displayed by checking for a specific element, such as a welcome message or dashboard header.

Step 4: Stop Recording

- Stop the recording in Selenium IDE and save the test case with an appropriate name, such as "TestLoginFunctionality."

Test Case 2: Dashboard Navigation

The second test case will verify that users can navigate to different sections of the dashboard after logging in. This test ensures that the links and buttons on the dashboard work as expected and that the user interface is responsive.

Step 1: Start Recording the Test Case

- Begin recording a new test case immediately after the login test case.
- Ensure that the application is on the dashboard page.

Step 2: Record Navigation Actions

- Click on various links or buttons on the dashboard to navigate to different sections, such as "Profile," "Settings," or "Reports."
- For each action, verify that the corresponding section or page is displayed by recording assertions that check for specific elements unique to those pages.

Step 3: Stop Recording

- Stop the recording once all navigation actions have been captured.
- Save the test case with a name like "TestDashboardNavigation."

Test Case 3: Form Submission

The third test case will focus on testing the form submission functionality within the dashboard. This test ensures that the form accepts input correctly, validates the input, and submits the data as expected.

Step 1: Start Recording the Test Case

- Start a new recording with the application on the form page of the dashboard.

Step 2: Record Form Input Actions

- Enter data into each field of the form, such as text boxes, drop-down menus, and checkboxes.
- For example, enter a name in the "Name" field, select an option from a drop-down menu, and check a checkbox for terms and conditions.

Step 3: Submit the Form

- Click the "Submit" button to submit the form.
- Record an assertion to verify that a confirmation message or a success page is displayed, indicating that the form was submitted successfully.

Step 4: Stop Recording

- Stop the recording and save the test case with a name like "TestFormSubmission."

Test Case 4: Logout Functionality

The final test case in our suite will verify the logout functionality. This test ensures that users can log out of the application and that they are redirected to the login page after logging out.

Step 1: Start Recording the Test Case

- Start recording a new test case from the dashboard or any page where the logout option is available.

Step 2: Record the Logout Action

- Click the "Logout" button or link to log out of the application.
- Verify that the application redirects to the login page by recording an assertion that checks for the presence of the login form.

Step 3: Stop Recording

Stop the recording and save the test case with a name like "TestLogoutFunctionality."

Assembling the Test Suite

After recording the four test cases, the next step is to assemble them into a test suite. In Selenium IDE, test suites are collections of test cases that can be run together, either sequentially or in parallel. This allows for comprehensive testing of the application's functionality in a single execution.

Step 1: Create a New Test Suite

- In Selenium IDE, create a new test suite and give it an appropriate name, such as "UserWorkflowTestSuite."

Step 2: Add Test Cases to the Test Suite

- Add the four recorded test cases to the test suite in the following order:
  1. TestLoginFunctionality
  2. TestDashboardNavigation
  3. TestFormSubmission
  4. TestLogoutFunctionality

Step 3: Configure Test Suite Settings

- Review the test suite settings and ensure that the tests will run in the correct order. You may also configure options for error handling, such as stopping the suite on failure or continuing with the next test case.

Executing the Test Suite

With the test suite assembled, the next step is to execute it and observe the results. Selenium IDE provides a play button to run the entire test suite, executing each test case in sequence. As the suite runs, Selenium IDE will highlight the steps being executed, and the results will be displayed in the log panel.

Analyzing Test Results

After the test suite execution, Selenium IDE will provide a summary of the results, indicating which test cases passed or failed. If any test case fails, the log will detail the step that caused the failure, along with any relevant error messages. This information is crucial for debugging and improving the test scripts.

Enhancing Test Cases

While the initial test suite provides basic coverage, it's important to continually enhance and refine the test cases to improve their robustness and reliability. Here are a few ways to enhance the test suite:

- **Parameterization:** Modify the test cases to accept parameters, allowing for the testing of different data sets without recording new tests. For example, you can parameterize the login credentials to test multiple user accounts.
- **Conditional Logic:** Add conditional statements to handle scenarios where the application behavior changes based on certain conditions, such as different user roles or varying form fields.
- **Error Handling:** Implement error handling to manage unexpected events, such as pop-up windows or loading delays. This can be done by adding wait commands or exception handling steps.

- **Test Suite Organization:** Organize the test suite by grouping related test cases together or by creating separate suites for different aspects of the application, such as functional tests, regression tests, and smoke tests.

Conclusion

Writing a test suite in Selenium IDE is a powerful way to automate the testing of web applications, especially for teams looking to create quick, reliable, and repeatable tests without the need for extensive coding. By recording user interactions and validating outcomes, Selenium IDE allows testers to build comprehensive test suites that cover a wide range of scenarios, from basic login functionality to more complex workflows like form submissions and navigation.

This case study of creating a test suite with four test cases—covering login, dashboard navigation, form submission, and logout—demonstrates the practical application of Selenium IDE in automating web testing. By following best practices, such as parameterization, error handling, and conditional logic, testers can enhance their test suites to ensure robust and reliable coverage of their applications.

As web applications continue to evolve, tools like Selenium IDE will remain essential for maintaining high-quality software through continuous testing and validation. Whether you're a beginner just starting with automation or a seasoned tester looking to streamline your workflow, Selenium IDE offers the flexibility and ease of use needed to keep pace with the demands of modern web development.

5.19. Conducting a Test Suite for Two Websites: A Comprehensive Approach

Conducting a test suite for two distinct websites involves a systematic process of defining, executing, and analyzing test cases that ensure each website's functionality, performance, and user experience meet the required standards. This process is crucial for identifying and addressing any issues that could affect the usability or reliability of the websites. The following is an in-depth explanation of how to conduct a test suite for two websites, covering the planning, execution, and analysis phases.

1. Understanding the Websites Under Test

Before developing a test suite, it's essential to gain a deep understanding of the websites being tested. This includes understanding their purpose, target audience, key functionalities, and the technologies used in their development.

Website 1: E-Commerce Platform

The first website in our test suite is an e-commerce platform designed to sell products online. The key functionalities of this site include product browsing, a search feature, shopping cart management, user authentication, and a payment gateway for transactions. The site may also feature user reviews, order tracking, and promotional offers.

Website 2: Educational Portal

The second website is an educational portal that provides online courses and learning resources. Its primary functionalities include course browsing, enrollment management, interactive lessons, user profiles, and progress tracking. This site may also feature discussion forums, quizzes, and certificates upon course completion.

2. Planning the Test Suite

The planning phase involves defining the scope, objectives, and specific test cases for the test suite. For both websites, the test suite should cover essential functionalities, edge cases, and scenarios that are likely to impact the user experience.

Test Objectives:

- **E-Commerce Platform:** Ensure the accuracy and reliability of the product catalog, the efficiency of the search functionality, the seamlessness of the shopping cart and checkout processes, and the security of the payment gateway.
- **Educational Portal:** Verify the accessibility and usability of course content, the accuracy of user progress tracking, the functionality of interactive elements like quizzes, and the reliability of the enrollment process.

Defining Test Cases:

For each website, the test cases should be categorized based on different aspects of the website's functionality. This categorization helps in organizing the test suite and ensures comprehensive coverage.

E-Commerce Platform:

- **User Authentication:** Test cases for registration, login, password recovery, and session management.
- **Product Catalog:** Test cases for product browsing, filtering, sorting, and detailed product pages.
- **Shopping Cart:** Test cases for adding and removing items, updating quantities, and viewing the cart.
- **Checkout Process:** Test cases for entering shipping details, applying discount codes, selecting payment methods, and completing the purchase.
- **Payment Gateway:** Test cases for processing payments with various methods, handling payment failures, and generating order confirmations.

User Reviews: Test cases for submitting, editing, and deleting reviews, as well as verifying review visibility.

Educational Portal:

- **Course Browsing:** Test cases for navigating course categories, viewing course details, and searching for specific courses.
- **Enrollment Process:** Test cases for enrolling in free and paid courses, unenrolling, and viewing enrollment status.
- **Interactive Lessons:** Test cases for accessing and interacting with lessons, completing quizzes, and submitting assignments.
- **User Progress:** Test cases for tracking lesson completion, viewing grades, and generating progress reports.
- **Discussion Forums:** Test cases for posting in forums, replying to threads, and managing notifications.

3. Executing the Test Suite

Execution involves running the test cases on both websites using automated or manual testing methods. The choice of testing method depends on the complexity of the test cases and the tools available.

Automated Testing with Selenium:

Selenium is a popular tool for automating web application testing. It allows testers to create scripts that simulate user interactions with the website, making it ideal for repetitive and complex test cases. For example, test cases involving user authentication, product browsing, and payment processing on the e-commerce platform can be automated using Selenium WebDriver.

Manual Testing:

While automated testing is efficient, some test cases require manual execution, especially those that involve subjective elements like user interface design or content accuracy. For the educational portal, manual testing might be necessary for verifying the clarity of instructional content, the usability of interactive lessons, and the responsiveness of discussion forums.

Parallel Execution:

To optimize the testing process, the test cases for both websites can be executed in parallel. This approach saves time and resources, especially when using cloud-based testing platforms that support concurrent test executions on different browsers and devices.

4. Analyzing Test Results

Once the test suite has been executed, the next step is to analyze the results. This involves reviewing the outcomes of each test case, identifying any failures, and determining the root causes of those failures.

Test Reporting:

A detailed test report should be generated for both websites, highlighting the success or failure of each test case. The report should include screenshots, logs, and error messages where applicable, providing a clear picture of the issues encountered during testing.

Issue Categorization:

Issues identified during testing should be categorized based on their severity and impact on the user experience. Critical issues, such as payment failures on the e-commerce platform or broken enrollment processes on the educational portal, should be prioritized for immediate resolution.

Root Cause Analysis:

For each failure, a root cause analysis should be conducted to determine the underlying reason for the issue. This analysis helps in developing targeted fixes and prevents similar issues from recurring in the future.

Regression Testing:

After the issues are resolved, regression testing should be conducted to ensure that the fixes have not introduced new problems. This involves re-running the relevant test cases and possibly extending the test suite to cover additional scenarios.

5. Continuous Improvement and Optimization

Testing is an ongoing process, especially for websites that are frequently updated or expanded. The test suite should be continuously improved and optimized based on feedback, new features, and evolving user requirements.

Test Suite Maintenance:

As the websites evolve, the test suite needs to be updated to reflect new functionalities, changes in user flows, and updated content. Regular maintenance of the test suite ensures that it remains relevant and effective.

Performance Testing:

In addition to functional testing, performance testing should be integrated into the test suite to assess how the websites perform under various conditions, such as high traffic or limited resources. Tools like JMeter can be used to simulate different load scenarios and measure the websites' responsiveness and stability.

User Acceptance Testing (UAT):

Before deploying significant updates or new features, User Acceptance Testing (UAT) should be conducted to validate that the websites meet the end-users' expectations. UAT involves real users interacting with the website in a controlled environment, providing valuable insights into usability and functionality.

Integration with CI/CD Pipelines:

For websites that follow a continuous delivery model, the test suite should be integrated into the Continuous Integration/Continuous Deployment (CI/CD) pipeline. This integration ensures that automated tests are run with every code commit, identifying issues early in the development process and reducing the risk of deploying faulty code to production.

5.20. Writing and Testing a Program to Login to a Specific Web Page: A Comprehensive Guide

Automated web testing is an essential practice in modern software development, allowing developers and testers to ensure the reliability, functionality, and security of web applications. One of the most common scenarios for automated testing is the login functionality, which is often the gateway to accessing various features of a web application. In this guide, we will explore the process of writing and testing a program to automate the login process for a specific web page, using Selenium WebDriver. The explanation will cover everything from setting up the testing environment to writing the script, executing it, and analyzing the results. By the end of this guide, you should have a comprehensive understanding of how to automate login testing for any web application.

1. Introduction to Selenium WebDriver

Selenium WebDriver is one of the most widely used tools for automating web application testing. It provides a programming interface to create and execute test scripts that interact with web elements, such as buttons, text fields, and links, in the same way a human user would. WebDriver supports multiple programming languages, including Java, Python, C#, and Ruby, and is compatible with various browsers like Chrome, Firefox, Safari, and Edge.

One of the key features of Selenium WebDriver is its ability to perform cross-browser testing, allowing the same script to be executed on different browsers to ensure consistent behavior. This makes Selenium an invaluable tool for web developers and testers aiming to maintain high-quality web applications.

2. Setting Up the Testing Environment

Before we can write and test a program to automate the login process, we need to set up our testing environment. This involves installing the necessary software and libraries, choosing a programming language, and configuring the WebDriver.

2.1. Installing Selenium WebDriver

The first step is to install Selenium WebDriver. Depending on your programming language of choice, the installation process may vary. For instance, if you're using Python, you can install Selenium via pip, the Python package manager:

bash

Copy code

```
pip install selenium
```

For Java, you'll need to download the Selenium Java bindings and include them in your project's dependencies, typically managed through a build tool like Maven or Gradle.

2.2. Choosing a WebDriver

Next, you'll need to download the WebDriver for the browser you intend to use. For example, if you're testing on Google Chrome, you'll need to download the ChromeDriver. Other options include GeckoDriver for Firefox and SafariDriver for Safari. These WebDrivers act as a bridge between Selenium and the browser, allowing your scripts to control browser actions.

2.3. Setting Up the Browser

After downloading the WebDriver, place it in a directory included in your system's PATH, or specify the path directly in your script. For example, in Python, you can set up the ChromeDriver as follows:

python

Copy code

```
from selenium import webdriver
# Specify the path to the ChromeDriver
driver = webdriver.Chrome(executable_path='/path/to/chromedriver')
```

This command launches a new Chrome browser instance that Selenium can control.

3. Writing the Login Automation Script

With the environment set up, we can now write the script to automate the login process. The script will navigate to the login page, enter the necessary credentials, submit the form, and verify the successful login by checking the presence of a specific element on the subsequent page.

3.1. Navigating to the Login Page

The first step in the script is to navigate to the web page where the login form is located. This is done using the get method of the WebDriver, which loads the specified URL in the browser:

python

Copy code

```
driver.get("https://www.example.com/login")
```

Here, replace "https://www.example.com/login" with the actual URL of the login page.

3.2. Locating Web Elements

Next, we need to locate the web elements corresponding to the username and password fields, as well as the login button. Selenium provides several methods for locating elements, including:

- find_element_by_id: Locates elements by their HTML id attribute.
- find_element_by_name: Locates elements by their name attribute.
- find_element_by_xpath: Locates elements using XPath expressions.
- find_element_by_css_selector: Locates elements using CSS selectors.

For example, to locate the username and password fields:

python

Copy code

```
username_field = driver.find_element_by_id("username")
password_field = driver.find_element_by_id("password")
```

These commands assume that the id attributes of the fields are "username" and "password." You'll need to adjust these values based on the actual attributes used on the web page.

3.3. Entering Credentials

With the fields located, the next step is to enter the username and password into the respective fields. This is done using the send_keys method:

python

Copy code

```
username_field.send_keys("your_username")
password_field.send_keys("your_password")
```

Replace "your_username" and "your_password" with the actual login credentials you want to test.

3.4. Submitting the Form

After entering the credentials, we need to submit the login form. This can be done by either locating and clicking the login button or by simulating a press of the Enter key:

python

Copy code

```
login_button = driver.find_element_by_id("loginButton")
login_button.click()
```

Alternatively, you can submit the form by sending the Enter key to one of the input fields:

python

Copy code

```
password_field.send_keys(Keys.RETURN)
```

3.5. Verifying the Login

Once the form is submitted, the script should verify that the login was successful. This typically involves checking that a specific element, such as a user profile link or a logout button, is present on the page:

python

Copy code

```
try:
profile_link = driver.find_element_by_id("profileLink")
print("Login successful!")
except NoSuchElementException:
print("Login failed.")
```

In this example, the presence of an element with id="profileLink" is used to verify the login. If the element is not found, the script assumes that the login failed.

4. Enhancing the Script with Error Handling and Reporting

While the basic script covers the fundamental steps of the login process, it can be further enhanced with error handling, reporting, and other features to make it more robust and useful in a real-world testing scenario.

4.1. Adding Error Handling

Error handling is crucial in automated testing to ensure that the script can gracefully handle unexpected situations, such as network errors, element changes, or incorrect credentials. You can use try-except blocks in Python to catch and manage exceptions:

python

Copy code

```
try:
driver.get("https://www.example.com/login")
username_field = driver.find_element_by_id("username")
password_field = driver.find_element_by_id("password")
username_field.send_keys("your_username")
password_field.send_keys("your_password")
```

```
login_button = driver.find_element_by_id("loginButton")
login_button.click()
profile_link = driver.find_element_by_id("profileLink")
print("Login successful!")
except NoSuchElementException as e:
print(f"Element not found: {e}")
except WebDriverException as e:
print(f"WebDriver error: {e}")
finally:
driver.quit()
```

The finally block ensures that the browser is closed at the end of the script, even if an error occurs.

4.2. Implementing Assertions

Assertions are used to validate that the test results meet the expected outcomes. For example, you can assert that the profile link is present after logging in:

python

Copy code

```
assert profile_link.is_displayed(), "Profile link not found, login might have failed."
```

If the assertion fails, the script will raise an error, indicating that the test did not pass.

4.3. Generating Test Reports

For larger projects, generating test reports is important for tracking the success and failure of different test cases. Tools like unittest in Python or JUnit in Java can be integrated with Selenium to create detailed test reports:

python

Copy code

```
import unittest
class LoginTest(unittest.TestCase):
defsetUp(self):
self.driver = webdriver.Chrome(executable_path='/path/to/chromedriver')
self.driver.get("https://www.example.com/login")
deftest_login(self):
driver = self.driver
```

```
username_field = driver.find_element_by_id("username")
password_field = driver.find_element_by_id("password")
username_field.send_keys("your_username")
password_field.send_keys("your_password")
login_button = driver.find_element_by_id("loginButton")
login_button.click()
profile_link = driver.find_element_by_id("profileLink")
self.assertTrue(profile_link.is_displayed(), "Login failed or profile link not found.")
deftearDown(self):
self.driver.quit()
if __name__ == "__main__":
unittest.main()
```

This script integrates Selenium with unittest, allowing you to run the login test as part of a larger test suite and generate reports on the results.

5. Executing the Test Script

With the script ready, the next step is to execute it and observe the results. You can run the script from your IDE, terminal, or CI/CD pipeline, depending on how your testing environment is set up.

5.1. Running Locally

To run the script locally, simply execute the Python file or run the test from your IDE:

bash

Copy code

```
python login_test.py
```

As the script runs, you should see the browser open, navigate to the login page, enter the credentials, and attempt to log in. The script will then print the result to the console, indicating whether the login was successful.

5.2. Running in a CI/CD Pipeline

For continuous integration, you can add the script to your CI/CD pipeline, where it will run automatically whenever new code is committed. This ensures that the login functionality is consistently tested and that any issues are caught early in the development process.

6. Analyzing the Results and Debugging

After executing the script, it's important to analyze the results to ensure that the test behaved as expected. If the script fails, debugging is necessary to identify and fix the issue.

6.1. Reviewing Logs and Screenshots

If your script includes logging or takes screenshots upon failure, reviewing these can provide valuable insights into what went wrong. Selenium can be configured to take screenshots when exceptions occur, which can be extremely helpful for debugging:

```
python
Copy code
driver.save_screenshot('screenshot.png')
```

6.2. Debugging Common Issues

Common issues with login scripts include incorrect element locators, timing issues (where elements aren't available when the script tries to interact with them), and changes to the web page's structure. Using explicit waits can help address timing issues:

```
python
Copy code
from selenium.webdriver.common.by import By
from selenium.webdriver.support.ui import WebDriverWait
from selenium.webdriver.support import expected_conditions as EC
# Wait until the element is present
username_field = WebDriverWait(driver, 10).until(
EC.presence_of_element_located((By.ID, "username"))
```

This code waits up to 10 seconds for the username field to appear before proceeding.

7. Expanding the Test Suite

Once the basic login script is working, you can expand your test suite to cover additional scenarios, such as:

- **Invalid Credentials:** Test how the application handles incorrect usernames or passwords.
- **Multi-Factor Authentication:** If the site uses multi-factor authentication (MFA), test the additional steps required to complete the login.

- **Different User Roles:** Test logins for different types of users, such as administrators, regular users, and guests.
- **Cross-Browser Testing:** Execute the script on different browsers to ensure consistent behavior across all platforms.

8. Conclusion

Automating the login process for a specific web page using Selenium WebDriver is a fundamental yet powerful capability that can significantly improve the efficiency and reliability of web application testing. By setting up a robust testing environment, writing well-structured and error-resistant scripts, and integrating the tests into your development pipeline, you can ensure that the login functionality—and by extension, other critical features—remains reliable throughout the development lifecycle.

This comprehensive guide provides a step-by-step approach to writing and testing a login automation script, covering everything from basic setup to advanced features like error handling, assertions, and reporting. With these tools and techniques, you can create a powerful and scalable test suite that not only validates the login process but also enhances the overall quality of your web application.

INDEX